GOD'S WILL *for* YOUR *earthly* RICHES

Why you must defeat poverty, make
more money, and touch more lives

Emmanuel Idu

ISBN: 94-92018-00-4
ISBN-13: 978-94-92018-00-7

Published by

Emmanuel Idu
INTERNATIONAL

EmmanuelIdu.org

Dedication

To everyone working hard to make ends meet and to those determined
to make the world a better place by advancing God's purpose through
the Gospel of our Savior and Lord Jesus Christ.

GOD'S WILL FOR YOUR EARTHLY RICHES

Contents

Acknowledgement

With gratitude to God for His continued inspirations from the Bible, to my precious wife, Irene, and to our daughters, Caroline and Darielle, for allowing me the time to write, and to our churches, friends and ministry partners around the world for their continued prayerful support.

Emmanuel Idu

Preface

What does God think about material riches? Can we have earthly riches without becoming materialistic? Can we desire and create material wealth without falling from the faith? Is it possible to enjoy riches in this life and still enjoy eternity with God? Does money have any eternal value? Can we have a balanced approach on the subject of worldly riches?

With fervent zeal for purity, fear of temptations, fear of persecution, and a deep dread for materialistic lifestyles, many honest but ill-informed Christians are embracing poverty and mediocrity and living below God's financial plans for His people.

Others, determined to be rich, are ignoring important principles of the Bible, and end up trading the fear of the Lord for material prosperity.

Consequently, we have a divided church with contradicting views that is slowing down the progress of God's work.

A third school of thought tries to avoid the controversy by staying away from the subject of money and claiming that it is not important.

The reality is that believers are spending an average of eight hours a day, five days a week, and about forty years of their precious lives trying to make money in order to pay their rent, buy cars and clothes, finance their homes, sponsor the education of their children, and support their churches. They are working hard to take care of some practical and material needs in their earthly lives. This shows the importance of money.

The fact is that many believers all over the world want to make significant financial contributions towards great causes in support of orphans, widows, churches, and other noble initiatives but often end up praying for the Lord to send help through other people because they themselves are financially weak.

Church boards spend hours brainstorming on how to meet financial challenges and advance the cause of Christ. This underscores the importance of money.

The time has come for us to address the subject more thoroughly and let the Bible speak!

God's Will for Your Earthly Riches will take you back to the Bible for answers that will defy popular opinions on the subject of wealth creation, money, and earthly riches. You can now discover why God wants you to grow richer and build more wealth than you will ever need in your lifetime.

1

WHY BELIEVERS MUST NEVER PROMOTE POVERTY

"The rich man's wealth is his strong city: the destruction of the poor is their poverty" (Prov. 10:15).

Wealth provides strength, and poverty can lead to destruction! God's own word has it in writing as you can read from the Bible verse above. In this very first chapter of the book, we shall examine reasons why we must never embrace, defend, or promote poverty - ever again!

Poverty is a prolonged state of lack or deficiency. It forces people to live below essential provisions in life. It frequently leads to weak performance and shaky results on projects. Poor people often have low self-esteem and low expectations. They regularly find themselves dreaming of the most basic things of life, such as nutritious food, decent shelter, and clothing because their limited financial situations make greater dreams appear unattainable.

Poverty keeps people preoccupied with the need to survive and makes it difficult for them to hold on to bigger dreams and a vision. It can make a person feel disadvantaged, incapable, rejected, and even miserable. The poor person's mind is hardly free to explore possibilities for greater accomplishments.

God wants His children to move forward, beyond survival, to the place where they would be able to meet the needs of others and transform lives for His glory. Poverty hinders God's wishes for His children.

The time has come for a change!

It is sad to see that many in our churches today are exalting and glorifying poverty, praising it as a sure way to attain purity and holiness. They condemn material riches, treat rich people with suspicion, and assume that God wants His people to stay away from money. Thus, they increase the hold of poverty on God's people by making them feel that poverty has special advantages.

With many church leaders ignoring the importance of comprehensive and practical financial education in the church, God's children are encouraged to stay poor and "humble" and to stay away from money because it is "the root of all evil"! (misquoting a selected portion of 1 Tim. 6:10).

Ironically, when believers are in financial need, our churches encourage them to believe God for financial breakthroughs and instruct them to expect miracles in areas where we should have taught them how to develop and use their God-given power to create wealth in abundance.

Although we serve a God of wonders, it is important to know that there are places and situations for miracles and divine interventions. The truth is that God never intended for miracles to replace our own efforts in carrying out our responsibilities. He expects us to make use of the gifts, talents, knowledge, and other qualities in our lives for our progress and the progress of His work. Whenever God gives abilities, it becomes the responsibilities of those with such abilities to make things happen. God reserves miracles for situations beyond our abilities.

Refusal to develop and use our God-given abilities for creating wealth is a clear choice for material limitations. Many believers have untapped abilities for creating wealth while churches continue to pray to God for a financial miracle!

The church encourages believers to ask the Lord for financial breakthroughs in order to pay essential bills, take care of the poor, finance missions, sponsor workers, and touch our communities while at the same time discouraging God's people from making money and becoming rich. This is absurd, and God wants to change it!

Poverty has no special advantage. On the contrary, it places undue limitations on precious people with great potential. Poor students know the bad feeling of not being able to afford textbooks for school, the humiliation of using school uniforms that were overdue for replacement, the health risk of living on a monotonous diet, and the frustration of not being able to travel freely.

Poor people know the bad feeling of being in lack and having to pray "... give us this day our daily bread" (Matt. 6:11).

Ask anyone that has actually tasted real poverty and they will tell you that it is much better to wake up in the morning with fresh bread on the table than it is for one to have to pray for it. We are far more fruitful when we wake up thinking about how to make the world a better place than we are when we welcome a new day with our minds troubled by the day's needs and our stomachs empty, forcing our mouths to pray for something as basic as food.

The Lord Jesus did not teach "... give us this day our daily bread" to define or predict a future in which God's people will live and enjoy purity through poverty and a state of material lack. On the contrary, He taught the prayer to give hope to people in need of material provisions and to assure them that they can trust our Heavenly Father to provide for them daily.

Many around the world with good intentions are going through life with unnecessary frustrations, unable to do the great things that they dream of because they lack funding for such undertakings. Lack of money has a way of crippling people and turning their plans into mere wishes. Many couples fight and risk separation because of financial pressure. Most churches would be able to do more good things and transform their environments faster if they had more money.

Countless believers have deep desires to transform their world, but they lack the financial means to make their wishes come true. It is painful to see people with great hearts lack the means to do good things while others with an abundance of money have no hearts to touch lives beyond themselves! The time has come for everyone with a great heart to have great riches and for everyone with great riches to have a great heart!

It is sad to see how the exaltation of poverty in our churches today has resulted in many believers living below their financial potential and believing God for miracles in practical areas where those outside of the church succeed and excel without needing miracles. For many years, we have seen sincere Christians plagued with poverty mentality because of their fear of money. This is hurting the advancement of God's purpose in our time, and the time has come to change it!

While it is not uncommon for one to go through one or more phases in life when it is necessary to trust the Lord for the basic daily needs, the truth is that God definitely wants to take His children beyond such experiences to a place of abundance, "… a land flowing with milk and honey" (Ex. 3:8).

God does not promise poverty as a blessing to His children in any place in the Scriptures. On the contrary, He promised them riches. The word of God declares, "The blessing of the LORD, it maketh rich, and he addeth no sorrow with it" (Prov. 10:22). Poverty brings sorrow. We must denounce poverty and declare a holy war against it!

Give no place to "Poverty Mentality" in your life!

Poverty Mentality is a mindset aligned with a conscious or an unconscious acceptance of poverty as a part of one's life or destiny. In the church, people spiritualize and accept this mentality by embracing poverty as God's plan for their lives. It is a way of thinking that makes them pursue the lowest standard in material things.

Such people, in their spiritual zeal, embrace things of the least quality as part of "humility" and consider poverty as a necessary part of life for any person in love with "purity." They criticize those seeking greatness in God and accuse them of being materialistic, worldly, proud, arrogant, ambitious, and selfish.

Poverty Mentality makes people detest riches and have suspicious attitude towards rich people. They feel that Christians only have their riches stored up for them in Heaven and insist that the believer is only in this world as a stranger to do God's work and "suffer for Jesus"!

They speak as if earthly riches are against God's work. The truth of the matter is that earthly riches have always facilitated God's work when in the hands of those with the right hearts. God's children must prosper in order to expand His work (Zec.1:17).

Beware of wrong interpretations of Bible passages!

Most of those exalting poverty in the churches refer to certain passages in the Bible in their efforts to defend their opinions on the subject. However, a careful examination of such passages will easily show that their assumptions are out of context. Let us see some of those passages.

1. *"Lay not up for yourselves treasures upon earth, where moth and rust doth corrupt, and where thieves break through and steal: But lay up for yourselves treasures in heaven, where neither moth nor rust doth corrupt, and where thieves do not*

break through nor steal: For where your treasure is, there will your heart be also" (Matt. 6:19–21).

If read within context, this passage actually speaks about prioritizing Heaven over the earth. The Lord is saying that it is better to lay up treasures in Heaven and to have our hearts set on the things above. He is not saying that we have to avoid earthly riches. We will see later in this book why poverty does not guarantee anyone a place in Heaven and riches do not take people to Hell.

2. *"Love not the world, neither the things that are in the world. If any man love the world, the love of the Father is not in him. For all that is in the world, the lust of the flesh, and the lust of the eyes, and the pride of life, is not of the Father, but is of the world. And the world passeth away, and the lust thereof: but he that doeth the will of God abideth for ever"* (1 John 2:15–17).

The passage above is telling us to avoid having love for money on the scale that we love God. Money is on a much lower scale than God or even human beings. Therefore, we cannot love money the way that we love God or love people. Doing so will be idolatry, an insult to the true and living God, and would open the door for an ungodly lifestyle dominated by the lust of the flesh, the lust of the eyes, and the pride of life.

Money is nothing but a tool that we are to use in service to God, for people, and for the things that are more important in life than money itself. We simply need to know the importance of money as a tool, get a lot of it, and do what we have to do in this world - better, faster, greater, and more efficiently and effectively.

Riches can only harm those that do not live in the will of God. As for those committed to God's mandate for their lives, He actually intends to arm them with riches because He understands the power of such a weapon in this world. The passage does not forbid God's people from having material riches.

3. *"And having food and raiment let us be therewith content. But they that will be rich fall into temptation and a snare, and into many foolish and hurtful lusts, which drown men in destruction and perdition. For the love of money is the root of all evil: which while some coveted after, they have erred from the faith, and pierced themselves through with many sorrows"* (1 Tim. 6:8–10).

This passage promotes contentment and warns people against the danger of pursuing riches for the mere sake of having riches. Contentment is an attitude of satisfaction and thankfulness for the most basic things of life, a holy virtue. It helps us to control the constant and natural yearning to have more and more for selfish reasons. Contentment goes hand in hand with self-control.

For example, when it comes to food, a contented person eats for nourishment. A person that lacks contentment eats gluttonously and wastefully, demanding more because the food looks attractive and tastes delicious. The contented person can say "no" when the glutton only wants more and more food to the detriment of his own health. A contented person is more likely to think about the needs of other people.

This book is not about getting rich just for the sake of being rich. It is about having earthly riches in the way that God intends it for His people. He wants His children blessed so that He can bless others through them. It takes those blessed with material riches to be able to bless the people in material distress. We cannot give anything that we do not have. Therefore, the passage above is not against being rich in God's way. It actually lays the foundation for being able to use riches in the right way. Contentment allows us to use material riches for goals other than our own selfish desires.

Read a few verses further in the same chapter and you will see that there were rich believers among them in the church. This made it necessary for Paul the Apostle to give the instruction below:

"Charge them that are rich in this world, that they be not highminded, nor trust in uncertain riches, but in the living God, who giveth us richly all things to enjoy; That they do good, that they be rich in good works, ready to distribute, willing to communicate; Laying up in store for themselves a good foundation against the time to come, that they may lay hold on eternal life" (1 Tim. 6:17–19).

God does not oppose earthly riches. He simply wants His people to have a healthy attitude towards it. A good attitude goes beyond meeting one's desire for self-gratification. People with a healthy attitude towards riches have deep and sincere interest in the general wellbeing of all people and in the advancement of God's purpose on the earth.

We all agree that God wants his children to overcome temptations and to stay clean in the process of building material riches. However, using the passage to imply that God wants His children to stay away from material riches is certainly a wrong interpretation.

4. *"And Jesus looked round about, and saith unto his disciples, How hardly shall they that have riches enter into the kingdom of God!"* (Mark 10:23).

Many take this passage to mean that no one trying to be rich will enter Heaven. However, when read within context, the passage does not condemn riches. It simply says that it is hard for those holding to their riches too tightly to enter into the Kingdom of God. We have to read the context in order to understand the Lord's message properly.

Here is the context:

A rich young man approached the Lord Jesus, asking to know what he must do to inherit eternal life (Mark 10:17). The Lord reminded him of the need to follow the commandments (Mark 10:19). The young man responded: *"...Master, all these have I observed from my youth"* (Mark 10:20).

The Bible tells us further: *"Then Jesus beholding him loved him, and said unto him, One thing thou lackest: go thy way, sell whatsoever thou hast, and give to the poor, and thou shalt have treasure in heaven: and come, take up the cross, and follow me"* (Mark 10:21).

After hearing this, the young man felt sad and went back home, grieved, because he had many possessions. It was at this point that the Lord Jesus said, *"... How hardly shall they that have riches enter into the kingdom of God!"* (Mark 10:23).

The issue here is not the earthly riches that the young rich man possessed but his unwillingness to obey the Master. The Lord commanded him to go and sell them and distribute the proceeds to the poor in order to answer the call and follow the Lord.

The young man's problem here is that he held on to the riches too tightly and would rather disobey the Lord than let go of his material possessions. His attitude towards riches was the problem. It is clear from his reaction that his riches were a kind of idol in his life. He trusted in riches, and that kept him back from following the Lord. He held on to his riches in a way that caused him to disobey the direct instruction of the Master. That is where he failed. God wants His children to be rich, but He does not want riches to become idols in their lives.

Some argue that it would have been easier for him to follow the master if he was not so rich, thus blaming his riches for his response. The truth of the matter is that riches are not the only thing that can hinder people from obeying God.

People not hindered by money may disobey God for other reasons. For example, someone wanted to go and bury the dead before following the Master. Another one wanted to go and say "Bye" to his people before following Him (Luke 9:59–62). Those unwilling to go all the way with the Lord have no shortage of reasons and excuses for refusing to follow His instructions.

Therefore, we cannot solely blame riches for the refusal of the rich young man to obey the Lord. The Lord wants us to have possessions, but our possessions must never possess us. We belong to the Lord!

Like many Bible students today, the disciples of the Lord initially thought that He was condemning riches, but He clarified His earlier statement in order to make sure that they did not see the man's money as the issue. He showed them that the young rich man's problem was in the fact that he trusted in money and not in God.

Read the verse below and you will see it for yourself:

"And the disciples were astonished at his words. But Jesus answereth again, and saith unto them, Children, how hard is it for them that trust in riches to enter into the kingdom of God!" (Mark 10:24).

Notice that He meant *"them that trust in riches."*

The problem is not really in having riches. God simply does not want us to trust in riches, because doing so can lead to disappointment, pride, and even idolatry! Those that trust in their riches often find it more difficult to obey God. Our confidence should be in the Lord, and riches should serve as tools in our hands for fulfilling God's purpose.

Job certainly knew the danger of trusting in riches and

examined his life in this area during his great trial (Job 31:24–25). The book of Psalms has several references to support this fact (Ps.49:6–7, Ps. 52:7, Ps. 62:10). Many other Bible passages also speak against trusting in riches (Prov. 11:28, Prov. 23:5, Jer. 9:23). It is wrong to trust in material riches.

Now, let us return to the story and observe the interactions between the Lord and His disciples to have an even clearer understanding of the Lord's teaching on the subject.

Intimidated by what appeared to be the Lord's high standard, they asked, *"Who then can be saved?"* (Mark 10:26). The Lord then reassured them that salvation is possible through God:

"And Jesus looking upon them saith, With men it is impossible, but not with God: for with God all things are possible" (Mark 10:27).

Peter then said, *"Lo, we have left all, and have followed thee"* (Mark 10:28). The disciples had done what the rich young man refused to do. They left everything behind in order to follow the Master. Peter pointed out the difference between their attitude towards possessions and that of the young rich man who had just walked away from the opportunity to follow the Master.

This shows that Peter did not get the real message. He still thought that the issue was about possessions, but that was not it!

Serving God is not about leaving things or people behind just for the sake of leaving them. It is about having enough confidence, love, trust, and commitment towards God to be willing to do whatever He asks us to do, even if that means letting go of our precious material possessions.

True faith in God makes a person willing to give up anything for God. Our God is not against possessions per se. On the contrary, He wants to see His children live in abundance and become the subjects of admiration to the people of the world (Gen. 26:12–14).

We can hardly make any sacrifices for His sake without receiving His reward. In order to make His message about possessions clearer to Peter, the Lord spoke more plainly and guaranteed him that God would give a hundred fold of possessions back to them in return for their sacrifices *"now in this time,"* and in the time to come, eternal life!

Read these words attentively:

"And Jesus answered and said, Verily I say unto you, There is no man that hath left house, or brethren, or sisters, or father, or mother, or wife, or children, or lands, for my sake, and the gospel's, But he shall receive an hundredfold now in this time, houses, and brethren, and sisters, and mothers, and children, and lands, with persecutions; and in the world to come eternal life" (Mark 10:29–30).

We can therefore conclude that the rich young man, by walking away from the opportunity to follow the Lord Jesus, had just missed an opportunity to receive a hundred fold of his entire riches! He also denied himself the opportunity to experience an adventurous life with the Master. God never makes us walk away from something without having greater things ahead for us. The path of consistent obedience to God is always better for us.

The young rich man missed an excellent chance to pursue God's calling on his life and risked missing eternal life! Do not blame it on his riches. He was ignorant and materialistic and had no idea that he was walking away from greater riches!

As you will see later in this book, one can be rich without setting one's heart on riches. Abraham, Job, David, and more servants of God all had riches yet trusted in God above their material possessions.

It is also important to remember that materialism is not an exclusive problem with rich people. It is an attitude of the heart. Therefore, poor folks are susceptible to it as well. Take, for example, a man called Achan, one of the soldiers in the army of Israel in the days of Joshua. He was not rich, but he was materialistic (Josh. 7:1).

Poverty can actually push people to become materialistic, covetous, and wicked. Most of the robberies in the world today happen through people that feel compelled by poverty to do so. Poverty is simply bad, period!

2

WHY POVERTY IS NOT GOD'S WILL FOR YOU

"For the LORD thy God blesseth thee, as he promised thee: and thou shalt lend unto many nations, but thou shalt not borrow; and thou shalt reign over many nations, but they shall not reign over thee. If there be among you a poor man of one of thy brethren within any of thy gates in thy land which the LORD thy God giveth thee, thou shalt not harden thine heart, nor shut thine hand from thy poor brother: But thou shalt open thine hand wide unto him, and shalt surely lend him sufficient for his need, in that which he wanteth" (Deut. 15:6–8).

Our opening passage comes from God's instructions to the children of Israel about the Year of Jubilee - a time when they were to cancel debts owed them by their brethren.

Although God consistently spoke of the Promised Land as a place of riches, fertility, and abundance, where they would eat and be full, He still found it necessary to instruct them about how to treat their poor brethren.

They were all children of Abraham and heirs to the same promises and all had access to the same law book containing wisdom for success and unlimited progress in all areas of their lives, yet God knew that some of them would be poor! The natural question that follows then is, "Why should any one of them be poor and be in need of mercy from the other?" Some may wonder why God would allow some of His children to be poor while allowing others to be rich.

Poverty is not God's will for the true believer, but people can be poor for a variety of factors, such as personalities, places, mentalities, attitudes, circumstances, phases in life, and many other factors. While it is beyond the scope of this book to cover all of them, we shall look at some of them in this chapter. Identifying these factors can position you to possess your material possession in God much faster and to live up to His expectations for you.

Disobedience opens the door for poverty

Disobedience to God can lead to poverty. God designed His instructions to help us prosper in everything that we do. Disregarding God's word can lead to serious consequences, including poverty.

Here is how the Bible puts it:

"Now these are the commandments, the statutes, and the judgments, which the LORD your God commanded to teach you, that ye might do them in the land whither ye go to possess it: That thou mightest fear the LORD thy God, to keep all his statutes and his commandments, which I command thee, thou, and thy son, and thy

son's son, all the days of thy life; and that thy days may be prolonged. Hear therefore, O Israel, and observe to do it; that it may be well with thee, and that ye may increase mightily, as the LORD God of thy fathers hath promised thee, in the land that floweth with milk and honey" (Deut. 6:1–3).

As you can read from the passage above, God designed the instructions to help them fear Him so that they could obey His word in order for them to enjoy long life and prosperity in the land flowing with milk and honey (Deut. 28:1–13).

Obeying God leads to divine favor and divine provisions. The Bible says, *"If ye be willing and obedient, ye shall eat the good of the land"* (Is. 1:19).

When people neglect or reject God's word, they indirectly choose the opposite of His blessings and invoke on themselves the consequences of disobedience. Poverty is one such consequence (Deut. 28:14–45). This is *poverty by disobedience.*

Poor beginning

Some people are poor because they inherited it from their family lineage. If a poor man dies and leaves his children without valuable material inheritance, barring other factors, then such children are more likely to live in poverty. We can call it *poverty by inheritance.*

Take, for example, the widow who cried to Elisha for help:

"Now there cried a certain woman of the wives of the sons of the prophets unto Elisha, saying, Thy servant my husband is dead; and

thou knowest that thy servant did fear the LORD: and the creditor is come to take unto him my two sons to be bondmen" (2 Kings 4:1).

Her husband feared God but left her with debts and at the mercies of merciless creditors after his death. The Bible does not say enough about her husband's lifestyle, and we are not in a position to judge him, but it certainly must have been a painful experience for her to face such a predicament after the pain of losing her precious husband, a man of God for that matter!

Had the Lord not intervened through Elisha the prophet, the widow and her sons would have suffered the bitter consequences of poverty at the hands of tough creditors. Our God has a way of intervening in the darkest hours of our lives when we seek Him sincerely and fervently.

That is what the prophet's widow did, and it is encouraging to observe that God did not disappoint her. She ended up receiving a miracle and enjoying supernatural provisions. Her husband left her with no money, but poverty was not God's will for her, and it certainly is not God's will for you.

The woman's widowhood began in poverty, but the Lord intervened! Most people have to work harder than usual and pay higher prices before achieving greater things in life, and many of them never fully defeat poverty in their lifetime because they began their journey in poverty.

Therefore, they also end up leaving no inheritance for the generations after them, leading to the transfer of poverty from one generation to the next as their children end up having to fight similar battles in a continuous circle of material lack.

Once held by poverty, it takes proper education, wisdom,

consistency, determination, hard work, time, spirituality, and the special grace of God for a family to break free. This is why it is extremely important for us to leave an inheritance for generations to come, as we shall see later in this book.

Environmental factors

A person living in a dry land with little or no natural resources, no access to lucrative jobs, no access to commercial activities, and no connection to profitable ventures is more likely to be poor.

Those that spend their precious time hanging out with the wrong people can also end up in poverty. We tend to take on the prevailing qualities in the lives of the people that have the most profound influence on us.

The Bible says:

"He that walketh with wise men shall be wise: but a companion of fools shall be destroyed" (Prov. 13:20).

"Hear thou, my son, and be wise, and guide thine heart in the way. Be not among winebibbers; among riotous eaters of flesh: For the drunkard and the glutton shall come to poverty: and drowsiness shall clothe a man with rags" (Prov. 23:19–21).

It is more difficult for those growing up in ghettos with immorality and violence to become rich when compared with those growing up in richer and more positive neighborhoods. Can someone grow up in the ghetto and become rich? The answer is "Yes!" History has many success stories supporting the fact that people are able to defy their backgrounds and take charge of their future. However, such people must be ready to follow strong principles, trust God, and work hard because the wrong environment often makes the journey towards material riches an uphill battle.

Growing up in a healthy environment may not guarantee success, but it definitely facilitates it. One's environment does matter. Many honest people are in poverty today because of their environments and not because God wants them to be poor.

Natural disasters

Earthquakes, storms, wildfires, famines, plagues, and many other natural forces beyond human control can render many people, and sometimes an entire neighborhood, poor, destroying many years of hard labor and accumulated wealth within a short time. Victims can be poor for several years before they recover. In some cases, such people do not recover at all.

The Bible mentions famine in several places. Here is one of them:

"And there was a famine in the land: and Abram went down into Egypt to sojourn there; for the famine was grievous in the land" (Gen. 12:10).

Abram had to flee from his dwelling place in order to sustain his family and escape the threat of extreme poverty. We must all pray and trust God to spare us from such experiences, and we need to be ready to help people in such situations. However, even in such difficult times, God often works out ways to help His people progress.

We know that the Lord blessed Isaac with abundance during the time of famine (Gen. 26:1, 12–14). With God's direction, Egypt had food in abundance when Joseph was in charge of the harvest. Even in the toughest famines, God takes care of His people, and you can rest assured that poverty is not for you (Job 5:20–22, Prov. 10:3, Is. 33:14–16, Ps. 33:18–22, Ps. 37:18–19).

Human causes

Poverty can come from the actions or inactions of other people; for example, wars. Citizens of many countries are languishing in extreme poverty today despite the fact that their nations are highly blessed with abundance of natural resources, such as gold, diamonds, oil, and other resources. Such countries have great potential for lucrative national income, but citizens suffer because of prolonged wars resulting from the selfish interests of a relatively few people in positions of power.

The majority of people in a nation may also suffer in poverty because of poor distribution of natural resources and mismanagement by policy makers. Other factors include corruption in government, manipulation by external political powers and enemies of the land, unethical business practices such as hoarding in order to create artificial scarcity, price manipulation, denial of access to lucrative markets, and many other human activities that serve to enrich a handful people at the expense of the vast majority of the people.

Here is an example of poverty resulting from human causes:

"And it came to pass after this, that Benhadad king of Syria gathered all his host, and went up, and besieged Samaria. And there was a great famine in Samaria: and, behold, they besieged it, until an ass's head was sold for fourscore pieces of silver, and the fourth part of a cab of dove's dung for five pieces of silver. And as the king of Israel was passing by upon the wall, there cried a woman unto him, saying, Help, my lord, O king. And he said, If the LORD do not help thee, whence shall I help thee? out of the barnfloor, or out of the winepress? And the king said unto her, What aileth thee? And she answered, This woman said unto me, Give thy son, that we may eat him to day, and we will eat my son to morrow. So we boiled my son, and did eat him: and I said unto her on the next day, Give thy son, that we may eat him: and she hath hid her son. And it came to pass, when the king heard the words of the woman, that he rent his clothes; and he passed by upon the wall, and the people looked, and, behold, he had sackcloth within upon his flesh" (2 Kings 6:24–30).

It is sad to know that many hardworking and honest people in our world today live in poverty because of avoidable human causes. They suffer unnecessarily in life because of the failures of their fellow citizens and/or leaders. Yet we know that poverty is not God's will for you! The grace of God can cause His people to prosper even in the most corrupt countries of the world, and they do not need to be corrupt in order to experience God's abundance.

Bad habits

Certain lifestyles and character traits naturally lead to poverty. Those that consistently ignore the importance of exercising self-control normally waste useful resources and end up in poverty. Such people do not recognize the strategic moments to delay gratification and to make temporary sacrifices in the interest of their own future and that of those depending on them.

The book of Ecclesiastes teaches us that there is a time to every purpose (Eccl. 3). Those in the habit of engaging in pleasure when they are supposed to be working suffer lack in due time.

Here is how the Bible puts it:

"He that loveth pleasure shall be a poor man: he that loveth wine and oil shall not be rich" (Prov. 21:17).

There is a time to sow and a time to reap. Ignorant people find pleasure in eating up their seeds in the time to sow and eventually have no harvest! Everyone with a determination to succeed in life must know that there is a time to work and a time to play.

Those that choose to play when they should be working do so at the expense of their own future success and are likely to have serious regrets. Wastefulness, laziness, idleness, gluttony, drunkenness, and other similar bad habits can make people poor.

The Bible is consistent about the fact that bad habits lead to poverty! Here are some of the many portions of the Bible designed to discourage bad habits:

"Slothfulness casteth into a deep sleep; and an idle soul shall suffer hunger" (Prov. 19:15).

"For the drunkard and the glutton shall come to poverty: and drowsiness shall clothe a man with rags." (Prov. 23:21).

"He becometh poor that dealeth with a slack hand: but the hand of the diligent maketh rich. He that gathereth in summer is a wise son: but he that sleepeth in harvest is a son that causeth shame" (Prov. 10:4–5).

"Love not sleep, lest thou come to poverty; open thine eyes, and thou shalt be satisfied with bread" (Prov. 20:13).

"Go to the ant, thou sluggard; consider her ways, and be wise: Which having no guide, overseer, or ruler, Provideth her meat in the summer, and gathereth her food in the harvest. How long wilt thou sleep, O sluggard? when wilt thou arise out of thy sleep? Yet a little sleep, a little slumber, a little folding of the hands to sleep: So shall thy poverty come as one that travelleth, and thy want as an armed man" (Prov. 6:6–11).

God does not bless laziness, and our world certainly does not benefit from it. Anyone aspiring to be rich must be willing to overcome bad habits and follow time-proven principles.

Lack of proper education

Another reason for poverty is lack of proper education. The word "proper" is crucial here because many people are making the mistake of thinking that they simply need to be educated, in whatever field or form, and they will succeed in life. While those in the business of education would like us to believe this, nothing is further from the truth.

You may have heard people say that "knowledge is power" or "no knowledge is a waste," but when it comes to becoming rich, it is more appropriate to say "relevant knowledge is power."

Knowledge can be useless if not relevant to the needs in the marketplace. For example, it may be exciting to know the number of planets that we have in the sky, but that knowledge itself is useless to a person planning to start and operate a bakery business successfully. Therefore, that knowledge will not be worth the investment of someone aspiring to become a baker.

People invest a fortune to learn too many useless things today because they merely seek academic titles and paper credentials. Always remember that it is possible for one to have honorable titles and academic credentials and be broke financially!

This is not the time to study simply for the sake of having credentials. University degrees in the wrong field will not put food on a person's table, and higher academic titles will do nothing more than boost the ego of those bearing them unless they are in relevant fields.

Having an academic qualification in a field that is not in demand within a person's marketplace is useless for generating wealth and can lead to poverty. A professional with a simple certificate in an area in great demand may be making a lot of money while another person with higher degrees may apply for jobs only to receive polite rejection letters in return.

To possess our material riches in God, we must learn how to make money, multiply money, put money to work for us, preserve money, protect money, build strategic alliances, negotiate, communicate, build strong brands, package goods and services properly, market what we have, and much more! Most importantly, we must be skilled in areas that are in demand or have the potential to be in demand when we enter into the marketplace.

GOD'S WILL FOR YOUR EARTHLY RICHES

We make money when we serve our world and receive favorable and reasonable rewards for our contributions. To earn money, we have to contribute products, tools, services, ideas, value, opportunities, and entertainment to our world and receive appropriate payments in return for our useful contributions. Otherwise, poverty is almost a sure outcome. Since poverty is not God's will for you, it is important that you make the right investment in the right education.

Lack of proper entry into the right marketplace

One environment may appreciate a particular service more than another environment does. The skills that make a person rich in one society may keep another person poor in a different society. Some companies making millions of dollars in profit annually in some Western countries by taking care of pets and supplying animal products to pet owners would be poor if they operated in war-torn nations where pet ownership is an unaffordable luxury to most people.

In certain parts of the world, people find themselves eating up precious animals that people in other parts of the world consider pets and family members. They do this to survive or simply as a part of their traditional meals. Selling pet supplies in such places would prove to be a bad business idea. The skills that one society celebrates may not enjoy appreciation in another society. Access to the right marketplace is therefore essential for success.

Many people with great moneymaking ideas fail and end up poor, not because God does not want them to have material riches but because they operate in the wrong markets, far away from God's plans for them.

Timing is also an important factor in financial success. The profession that makes people rich in a given time may not have any special advantages in another time. For example, in the early years of the Internet revolution, people made good money operating Internet cafes in Western countries. Today, most of these cyber cafes are going out of business because the majority of the people now have Internet access through their mobile phones; the need to make use of Internet cafes has decreased significantly. The timing is no longer in favor of such a business.

There was a time when people made money as typists and computer operators. Others paid them to type letters and to carry out basic computer tasks, but in a world where people type their own letters and more people own their own computers and printers at home, there is no need for the professions of typists and computer operators. As more people learn to take care of their own computer operation needs, certified computer operators will become more redundant and in less demand. They must prepare to learn new trades and develop other skills to serve their world or move to another part of the world where demand may still exist for their current skills.

Poverty comes when there is lack of proper education in the right fields, for the right time. The right education, field, and time are those in demand in the marketplace where one has access.

We live in a time when most companies consider profit making more important than job creation, making them pay closer attention to the performance of their shares in the stock market. Global competition is more intense now than ever, and most of the companies operating today did not start up their businesses to become charity organizations. Therefore, anyone studying for gainful employment must be prepared to excel and enter the labor market with the knowledge and the skills that are in - or will be in - demand.

Since poverty is not the will of God for you, it is essential that you pay close attention to the qualities, goods, and services that you are bringing into the market place. The Lord wants you to be in demand.

Lack of effective business and financial education

Apart from studying incorrectly, many people also find themselves poor, irrespective of how much money they earn, because they lack proper financial and business education. Some people may win millions of dollars in a lottery and still end up in poverty in a few years because they lack the education necessary to manage and grow that kind of money.

The son of a wealthy entrepreneur may inherit a thriving business and still become poor because he lacks the character, expertise, determination, and other qualities responsible for the success of his father.

The Bible says,

"My people are destroyed for lack of knowledge: because thou hast rejected knowledge, I will also reject thee, that thou shalt be no priest to me: seeing thou hast forgotten the law of thy God, I will also forget thy children" (Hos. 4:6).

"The lips of the righteous feed many: but fools die for want of wisdom" (Prov. 10:21).

"Where there is no vision, the people perish: but he that keepeth the law, happy is he" (Prov. 29:18).

Anyone determined to progress in life cannot afford to lack proper business and financial education. Get the education that is required to help you possess, manage, and grow your portions of material riches in the Lord.

Disregard for riches

Money, earthly riches, and material prosperity are subjects that tend to turn off well-intended Christians in many quarters across several denominations today. Since we progress more naturally in the areas where we excel and we are more likely to excel in the areas of our interest or passion, many poor people suffer at the hands of poverty because of their lack of interest in material riches.

It is hard to work hard and succeed in any field that does not stir up interest or passion in us. We simply will not have the commitment and the faith necessary to press forward long enough to be able to see the kind of results that are necessary. We can only have faith in the things that we embrace. We can only build fire for the things that we believe in.

With much effort, one may succeed in taking an unwilling horse to a stream, but it is much harder to force such a horse to drink water! Most progressive people in life reached great goals because they *wanted* to do so. They had an interest in what they chose to do.

Try to imagine how frustrating it can be for an excellent coach to work hard to make someone an outstanding athlete if that person does not like participating in contests and consistently works against the intentions of the coach. That is how hard it can be to make people rich if they have no personal wishes to have material riches.

God requires us to have desires for the great things that He has in mind for us. In most cases when God performed miracles in the Bible, He did so in response to not only the needs of people but to their desires for such miracles.

Most Bible students know the story of the woman with the issue of blood. She touched the Lord Jesus and received instant healing. Let us take a quick look:

"And, behold, a woman, which was diseased with an issue of blood twelve years, came behind him, and touched the hem of his garment: For she said within herself, If I may but touch his garment, I shall be whole. But Jesus turned him about, and when he saw her, he said, Daughter, be of good comfort; thy faith hath made thee whole. And the woman was made whole from that hour" (Matt. 9:20–22).

This woman had a strong personal desire to experience healing and planned on how to receive it. She would have made no efforts if she had concluded her state to be acceptable and had embraced her pain as part of God's plans to keep her humble so that she could gain eternal life after the years of her suffering in this world. She would have had no faith for instant healing. Our faith usually travels in the direction of our deepest longings.

"Daughter, be of good comfort; thy faith hath made thee whole" was the Master's response to the woman.

Many other stories of miracles in the Bible are in line with the fact that recipients had personal desires for their miracles. Our faith can never exceed our desires! Those that oppose and reject material riches, abhor rich people, and downplay the importance of riches are more likely to live and die in poverty. You need to have a strong desire for the Lord's portion or plan of material riches for your life if you want to excel in His purpose.

Spiritual forces

We live in a time when there is little spiritual education, especially in the Western world. Many people find it difficult to believe anything that they are not able to experiment repeatedly in the laboratories. This makes it difficult for them to believe things that their analytical minds cannot comprehend. Consequently, they suffer under mysterious circumstances.

Modern society may try to downplay the spiritual aspect of life here on earth, but Bible students know that most of the things that we experience in the physical world have spiritual origins. There are unseen forces affecting the state of affairs in the known world.

The Bible's account of the life of Daniel can help to illustrate this point. He prayed to God and waited for about twenty-one days to receive the answer through an angel named Gabriel. God answered his prayer from the very day that he began praying, but it took longer than usual for the answer to reach him because an evil spiritual force referred to as the "prince of the kingdom of Persia" opposed the angel. Gabriel was only able to deliver the message to Daniel after obtaining assistance from another angel named Michael.

Here is the Bible passage:

"Then said he unto me, Fear not, Daniel: for from the first day that thou didst set thine heart to understand, and to chasten thyself before thy God, thy words were heard, and I am come for thy words. But the prince of the kingdom of Persia withstood me one and twenty days: but, lo, Michael, one of the chief princes, came to help me; and I remained there with the kings of Persia" (Dan. 10:12–13).

Another example is an instance in the life of Elisha, the prophet. This prophet had special spiritual abilities to see secrets. He used this special ability to reveal the movement of the enemy to the king of Israel. He exposed the movement of the enemy's forces several times, disrupting strategic battle plans in favor of Israel.

With time, the enemy concluded that they would only be able to defeat Israel if they could arrest the prophet. They sent out a team on a mission to capture the prophet. As they positioned themselves for his arrest, Elisha's servant feared for his life and that of the prophet, but Elisha remained calm. To help his servant overcome his fear, Elisha prayed to God to open the spiritual eyes of the young man, and the secret of Elisha's courage became obvious - they had invisible supernatural spiritual support! Here is how the Bible describes the incident:

"And when the servant of the man of God was risen early, and gone forth, behold, an host compassed the city both with horses and chariots. And his servant said unto him, Alas, my master! how shall we do? And he answered, Fear not: for they that be with us are more than they that be with them. And Elisha prayed, and said, LORD, I pray thee, open his eyes, that he may see. And the LORD opened the eyes of the young man; and he saw: and, behold, the mountain was full of horses and chariots of fire round about Elisha" (2 Kings 6:15–17).

The spiritual world is real, and God's word contains spiritual laws that we must learn to consider when making choices in life if we want to be free from adverse spiritual effects. Adverse spiritual influences can lead to poverty, failure, sicknesses, oppression, and much more.

God's power is at work to do well, while there are evil powers at work to do evil. The Bible says:

"For I know the thoughts that I think toward you, saith the LORD, thoughts of peace, and not of evil, to give you an expected end" (Jer. 29:11).

"The thief cometh not, but for to steal, and to kill, and to destroy: I am come that they might have life, and that they might have it more abundantly" (John 10:10).

A person walking in God's blessings will receive power to prosper and will live in abundance, while someone walking under curses will suffer under the adverse effects of evil forces, resulting in frequent misfortune, including poverty.

Curses can have negative consequences on a person's progress. Such effects may include poor harvest, ill health, defeats, and much more (Lev. 26:1–46). We can overcome the power of curses by staying under God's spiritual protection.

Spiritual matters have mysterious influences on lives. To remain spiritually healthy, one must walk in line with God's directions and stay under His protection. Anyone under curses must repent, turn to God, and embrace His purpose. Our God is merciful enough to forgive, deliver, restore, and protect those that turn to Him for help. Walk with the Lord, and no curse will be strong enough to prevent you from possessing your possessions.

Tongues of people

Apart from the curses that are the natural results of a person's doing, the enemy, in his evil intentions, often exercises spiritual powers by speaking out curses on individuals. Haters and envious people can release spiritual powers through their words or hire spiritual agents to do so. An example of this is the story of a king called Balak. He hired a spiritual man by the name of Balaam to curse the children of Israel (read Numbers 23 and 24).

However, King Balak's efforts failed because God intervened. The children of Israel were living in God's will at the time, and His protection was on their lives. As a result, the Lord turned the curses into blessings: *"Nevertheless the LORD thy God would not hearken unto Balaam; but the LORD thy God turned the curse into a blessing unto thee, because the LORD thy God loved thee"* (Deut. 23:5).

In another example, David was about to fight against Goliath. As he approached Goliath with staves, the giant felt insulted and then cursed David in the name of his gods: *"And when the Philistine looked about, and saw David, he disdained him: for he was but a youth, and ruddy, and of a fair countenance. And the Philistine said unto David, Am I a dog, that thou comest to me with staves? And the Philistine cursed David by his gods"* (1 Sam. 17:42–43).

Curses invoke spiritual laws and forces to act against a person, a place, an event, or a thing. By cursing David, the Philistine was preparing the way to defeat David spiritually before engaging him in a physical fight. However, Goliath failed because David was under the protection of the Most High God! At the end, David killed Goliath in that battle. David would have had grave consequences if he did not have divine protection from the Almighty God.

People can be poor for natural reasons, and they can be poor for spiritual reasons. Those poor for spiritual reasons may work hard and still see no sustained progress. The curses spoken on their lives must first be broken through the superior spiritual power of the Most High God. Feel free to pause and call on the Lord Jesus Christ right now if you sense that there are curses operating in your life because of some evil words spoken over you.

The Lord Jesus declares, *"If the Son therefore shall make you free, ye shall be free indeed"* (John 8:36).

The tongues of people can cause uncountable damage. Conscious of the damage that the tongue can do, the word of God teaches every child of God to condemn such tongues:

"No weapon that is formed against thee shall prosper; and every tongue that shall rise against thee in judgment thou shalt condemn. This is the heritage of the servants of the LORD, and their righteousness is of me, saith the LORD" (Is. 54:17).

Words are powerful, and you must never take them lightly. Examine the words spoken around you, and reject any declaration towards your life and the lives of the people under your care if such words are not in line with the will of God.

"Death and life are in the power of the tongue: and they that love it shall eat the fruit thereof"
(Prov. 18:21).

The conclusion

We have seen many possible causes of poverty, and none of them is in line with the will of God for your life. Poverty is not the Lord's plan for His children. Therefore, you must reject poverty in every form and embrace God's will for your material riches. Decide now to get your portion in this world so that you can fulfill your purpose in the Lord.

3

LEARN TO APPRECIATE THE GREAT POWERS OF MONEY!

"A feast is made for laughter, and wine maketh merry: but money answereth all things" (Ecc. 10:19)

Today, we measure material or earthly riches by their value in monetary terms. We say that a house is worth a certain amount of money in a given currency or that a person's net worth is up to a specific amount in a particular currency, such as the United States dollars.

For this reason, we shall be using "riches," "wealth," and "money" throughout this book to mean the same thing. Technically, these are not exactly the same. Money is the currency we use as a means of exchange in transactions. Riches refer to how much of it we have in excess. Wealth is how much of it we have accumulated in the form of treasure, fortune, or capital. However, we shall be using the terms interchangeably for ease of communication and in line with the goal of keeping this book as simple as possible. We will also be using the terms "material riches" and "earthly riches" interchangeably as well.

What will you do with excess money?

What will you do if you have far more money than you need for supporting a reasonable and comfortable lifestyle? It is hard for anyone to answer such a question for you. A thousand people can all have different answers to the question depending on how much money they have and their personal values, mindset, priorities, and many other factors. However, there is no doubt that you will have the *ability* or the *power* to *do* many good things if you choose to. This is because money is powerful! Power is the ability to get things done. Having excess money will make it possible for you to do more of the things that money can do.

What can money do? We live in a world where money can do a whole lot of things. With money, you can take good care of yourself and your family. You can sponsor your church, spread the Gospel around the world, feed the children suffering from malnutrition in many developing countries, support your favorite causes, create job opportunities, educate a new generation, buy time, and even buy new opportunities in life for you and for others! The list can go on indefinitely. This is why our opening passage says *"money answereth all things."*

In some countries, you can even influence the political contest by donating to the candidates representing the values that you stand for. As you may already know, many politicians win elections today not because they have the best policies or are the most qualified persons to govern but because they have the financial resources to pay for expensive election campaigns.

With enough money, you can buy your own media houses and influence public opinions in the direction of your mission in this life. With God, the right vision, the right people, and lots of money, you can influence and change your world! Why should anyone want to stay away from such a powerful tool?

Having excess money will give you enormous powers, and you can use these powers to do a great deal of good in your environment, around the world, and far beyond your generation. Money is powerful indeed!

Let us look closer at some of the powers of money:

Money gives you options

With enough money, you can pay people to do the things that you do not like to do, making you free to focus on doing those things that you are passionate about doing. Imagine a lifestyle that allows you to minimize your distractions and gives you opportunities to function more effectively. How productive would you be if someone would take away all of the time-wasting, routine activities of your daily life? One can bet that most people would be able to do far more than others have imagined. Money can make this possible for you.

Money presents you with several options and gives you power to choose from these options. You can choose which school to send your children to if lack of money does not stand in your way. You can choose which neighborhood to live in, which tasks to carry out by yourself, and which tasks to outsource to others. Having options gives you flexibility and positions you to follow your dreams with a higher level of concentration, thereby helping you to achieve your dreams more smoothly and, in many cases, faster!

If that dream is to follow God's plan for your life and to touch your world, then money will serve you well as a versatile tool. Get more money than you need, and your options will increase in many situations and places in this world. The ability to choose is a very important power!

Money gives you a voice

Whether you like it or not, people will judge you by your financial standing. We must admit this part of daily reality. Barring the suspicion and evidence of wrongdoing, people will naturally assume that you are smarter and wiser if they see you to be more successful or appearing to be more successful financially. They will tend to listen more attentively when you speak.

A rich person with little wisdom is more likely to get the attention of the crowd than the poor person is, even if such a poor person is wiser. Our world looks down on poor people.

While most of us will agree that it should not be so, we cannot deny the fact that rich people have more influence in our world today. They influence many political decisions behind the scenes - and sometimes openly. Many laws do not pass without considering their interests. People simply listen when they speak.

The Bible is clear about this fact. Read the following passage and see for yourself:

"There was a little city, and few men within it; and there came a great king against it, and besieged it, and built great bulwarks against it: Now there was found in it a poor wise man, and he by his wisdom delivered the city; yet no man remembered that same poor man. Then said I, Wisdom is better than strength: nevertheless the poor man's wisdom is despised, and his words are not heard" (Ecc. 9:14–16).

Notice there *"the poor man's wisdom is despised, and his words are not heard."* Wisdom without an audience leads to a life without influence! A wise person should have an audience in order to make a positive impact on lives. The larger the audience a person has, the greater the potential that such a person has for making a difference.

Therefore, it will do our world, and the Kingdom of God, greater good for wise and godly people to grow in material riches as they increase in wisdom. It is a great waste of potential and an abomination for a wise person to be poor in our present world.

I undermined money in the early years of my Christian life as I saw people willing to compromise their stand on holiness in order to get rich. However, as I began to see the needs of the world and to study the Bible on the subject of money more closely, it became obvious that I was judging money by the wrong attitude of people and neglecting a very significant, strategic, and powerful tool for doing God's work. I had to repent!

Money is a defense

Just like wisdom, money is a defense in this world.

The Bible says, *"For wisdom is a defence, and money is a defence: but the excellency of knowledge is, that wisdom giveth life to them that have it"* (Ecc. 7:12).

God is our ultimate defender, but there is a sense in which those with sufficient money have more material security than those that do not have money. Rich people often have food reserves in times of drought and usually have provisions for urgent situations. Spiritual security is extremely important, but we also need material security. Money provides material security.

Rich people have more resources for responding to the practical challenges of life and find it easier to respond to lawsuits, defend their rights, and secure their territories. Poor people often suffer abuse, neglect, and rejection by the world around them, often ending up as voiceless victims in an oppressive world. God does not want you to be a victim in this world. On the contrary, He wants you to be strong so that you can help those that are weak and vulnerable.

Have you noticed that rich people driving in cars that are more expensive tend to be safer in most densely populated cities with high traffic? I have been to many such places around the world and have noticed that most drivers keep more distance and drive more carefully around expensive cars. Such drivers are aware of the fact that it may cost them a lot of money to repair any damage inflicted on such automobiles. They also assume that such cars carry more important and influential people that are capable of defending their own rights. They are aware that hurting important people can have grave consequences because of the powers of such people.

Some people may argue that money makes one a target of crime and attracts robbers, thieves, kidnappers, and such criminals, but there is no record to prove that poor people are safer. Poor neighborhoods often experience heinous crimes, and it is common to find victims of robbery, rape, and other heartless crimes in such neighborhoods. The poor have no defense advantage over the rich in our natural world.

Have you also noticed that poor people tend to suffer more in times of sudden natural disasters? They usually build their houses with cheaper materials that are less equipped to handle the kind of high impacts that are associated with certain levels of storms, earthquakes, and other dangerous weather conditions. The rich find it easier to afford the high costs of purchasing land in prime locations, building their houses with the help of experts, and using better building materials, thereby increasing their natural defenses. Money is definitely a defense!

Money attracts people with special gifts and talents

Many people understand the power of money and seek opportunities to meet those that they believe have lots of money. If your world knows you to be rich, people with innovative ideas will come looking for you, and they will offer you opportunities for partnership in their effort to release their innovative ideas into the world.

People with great talents but lacking the financial resources to reach their dreams will look for the chance to meet with you and to present their ideas in the hope that you will be able to work with them and help to propel them into greatness. This will give you opportunities to help people, create jobs, improve quality of life, and grow more in material riches.

The more reasonable and generous you are, the more likely you are to attract some of the most talented people in this world. Money will force people with great ideas to chase you! If you have little money, you will find yourself looking for the right people to get things done, but the right people will be looking for opportunities to do things with you if your world knows that you have a lot of money. They will come to you with proposals for your approval! Do you prefer to run after people to get things done, or do you prefer to opportunities to run after you?

The Bible says,

"Many will intreat the favour of the prince: and every man is a friend to him that giveth gifts"
(Prov. 19:6).

People like to be around those that have solutions for their needs. Riches put you in the position to solve material problems and to meet practical needs, hence attracting people to you so that you can make positive contributions to their lives. This is extremely important if you feel that it is part of your mission in this life to make a positive difference in your world.

One may rightly argue that it is morally wrong to let people come close to us only for the sake of money. However, such an argument is weak because it denies an important reality in our world. The reality is that the average person is inherently selfish and seeks personal interests by default.

This is not a new thing. People were also like that in the days when the Lord Jesus Christ walked on this earth. Many of His followers went to Him because they wanted to receive healing, personal direction, deliverance, and miracles and to learn important lessons about the Kingdom. Some actually followed Him for physical food! Their motives were mostly selfish, but He did not turn them away. On the contrary, He used every opportunity to exercise godly influence on their lives.

His teachings brought them personal fulfillment and gave them hope of a better life here on earth and eternal life beyond this time. He was aware of their selfish motives, but that did not deter Him from receiving them and taking the time to teach them the Scriptures.

God knows man's selfishness and actually uses that knowledge to guide man on the right path. In the Old Testament, God promised blessings for obedience and curses for disobedience:

"Behold, I set before you this day a blessing and a curse; A blessing, if ye obey the commandments of the LORD your God, which I command you this day: And a curse, if ye will not obey the commandments of the LORD your God, but turn aside out of the way which I command you this day, to go after other gods, which ye have not known" (Deut. 11:26–28).

God was aware of man's natural tendencies to follow selfish motives, and He spoke in the language that appealed to the natural selfish motives of the people, promising blessings for obedience and curses for disobedience.

We live in a world where people consistently want to know what is in a cause for them before they go for it. Many take the time to look at the potential return on investment (ROI) in most of their undertakings. Do not let this fact bother you. On the contrary, take advantage of it for the prosperity of God's Kingdom.

Being rich gives you the power to make things work for others, and they are aware of it. You need to be aware of this fact as well. Be rich, and you will matter more! Half an hour with you may change their lives forever. A recommendation letter from you may land someone a lucrative job. A phone call by you may result in a business opportunity for a hardworking young entrepreneur.

Riches definitely give one earthly powers, and the world knows it. This is why they will pay money to attend special business dinners just to be able to exchange business cards with one or more strategic influencers.

Put your concerns about people's selfishness to rest with the understanding that they eventually begin do things with higher and less personal motives in mind after experiencing God and discovering the power of His love.

Until such a time when the leading motive behind their choices in life becomes their love for God and for others, we must be conscious of their selfish conditions in our plans to influence them in the will of God. With man's selfishness in mind, we must choose money and riches over poverty and lack in order to touch our world for God!

Poverty makes people want to stay away from a person because poor people can be a burden to others. The Bible is clear about this human inclination:

"All the brethren of the poor do hate him: how much more do his friends go far from him? he pursueth them with words, yet they are wanting to him" (Prov. 19:7).

"Wealth maketh many friends: but the poor is separated from his neighbour" (Prov. 19:4)

"The poor is hated even of his own neighbour: but the rich hath many friends" (Prov. 14:20).

It is certainly better to be in a position where people seek your favor than to live at a level where people despise you and try to avoid you. God wants His children to be attractive. God certainly wants you to lead your trade - and your world!

Most of us know that true believers are supposed to live in spiritual power with the anointing and faith to heal the sick, set free those that are in spiritual bondage, and perform miracles in the name of the Lord Jesus Christ, but we often forget the importance of operating in the power of material riches as well. God wants us to be able to feed those that are hungry, to give shelter to those that are homeless, and to create opportunities for progress to those that are suffering in this world.

We need to serve God with the awareness that He is interested in the total welfare of man and not only in their spiritual wellbeing. The Lord Jesus drove out evil spirits, healed the sick, raised the dead, and taught many important lessons, but he also gave food to the crowd when they were hungry.

Riches increase courage

Many people would achieve more in their lives if they were less fearful and more courageous. Poverty has a way of making one insecure, fearful, and timid. Progressive people are often bolder and more courageous. Courage comes through confidence. Without confidence in something, in oneself or in someone else, life will be intimidating, and we will avoid taking many of the bold steps that are essential for greater achievements.

While our ultimate confidence should be in God, the fact remains that courage can come in many ways. For example, in times of false accusation, a person with a clean conscience can be courageous. Therefore, purity gives courage. On the day of examination, students that understand the content of their academic materials can go into examination halls with more confidence, while others may be nervous and fearful. This shows that knowledge can bring courage.

A person well trained in self-defense is more likely to be courageous when walking through a lonely street at night than one that is not. This shows that being skilled and strong can increase a person's courage. Money increases courage.

Stronger nations act with more confidence than weaker nations on the global stage. This may help to explain why many nations want to grow richer and have stronger weapons of war. They want to be significant in order to have a stronger voice, to deter aggression from any other nation that may want to take undue advantage of them, and to increase their global advantage.

In the same way, a wealthy person is more confident in life when confronted with situations that money can handle. Rich people have less to worry about in times of minor price increases in essential commodities. They do not see the need to resort to violent demonstrations and risk reprisals from strict authorities before having their voices heard. They can sleep well at night knowing that such minor price increases will not cause their world to fall apart.

Money is certainly not the only source of confidence. As mentioned earlier, there are other ways to feel confident even when one does not have money. Wisdom gives confidence. Faith gives confidence. A person with faith can move around through dangerous places with courage, trusting in God's divine protection. In a time of material needs, such a person can trust

God for supernatural provisions. One may have no money and still have more courage than those with enough money to last for several generations. Notwithstanding, money is powerful indeed, and it is clear that money's power gives confidence.

In looking at the power that money brings, we must also remember that power, although good, can be dangerous when not properly managed. It has the potential to corrupt a person's character and result in an unhealthy attitude towards others.

The Bible says, *"The poor useth intreaties; but the rich answereth roughly"* (Prov. 18:23).

Money can make a person become proud, arrogant, power-drunk, abusive, and oppressive, attracting God's anger and punishment. Rich people can feel that they know better than other people and become less open to correction, leading to their own downfall. They may start building their confidence and hope in money and feel no need for God, resulting in a pitfall.

Money can create the illusion that the rich are untouchable, resulting in sudden destruction. Anyone with a lot of money must engage in regular self-examination and reality checks in order to ensure spiritual and character health.

Does this mean that money is bad? No! Must we then fear money? No! In itself, money has no moral character and cannot be bad or good in any moral sense. It takes on the character of the owner. We can use power for good or for bad depending on our character and the leading motives for wielding the power in our hands. People with evil intentions can use power wrongly and cause pains to others and to themselves, but we must never let the fear of misusing power deprive us of the powers that we need in life. People with good intentions can do countless good things with the power of money in their hands if they develop solid character and live with integrity.

Power, in any form, whether it is money, knowledge, or in some other form, can corrupt those that lack the character foundations necessary for operating with them.

For this reason, the Bible also warns against the danger of the power of knowledge:

"Now as touching things offered unto idols, we know that we all have knowledge. Knowledge puffeth up, but charity edifieth" (1 Cor. 8:1).

This means that knowledge has the tendency to puff a person up. In other words, it can make a person proud and arrogant.

The Bible says, *"Pride goeth before destruction, and an haughty spirit before a fall"* (Prov. 16:18).

Should we then embrace ignorance and stay away from knowledge in order to avoid pride, be more humble, and prevent a fall? No! On the contrary, we need knowledge to stand, and the Bible encourages us to grow in knowledge (2 Pet. 3:18, Eph. 1:17, Col.1:10).

To reject or neglect knowledge implies that we would live in ignorance. The Bible is very clear about how dangerous this can be:

"My people are destroyed for lack of knowledge: because thou hast rejected knowledge, I will also reject thee, that thou shalt be no priest to me: seeing thou hast forgotten the law of thy God, I will also forget thy children" (Hos. 4:6).

If knowledge is dangerous and ignorance is dangerous, then one may ask, "What shall we do then?" The answer is obvious: we simply have to make sure that we build the character necessary to carry the amount of knowledge that we possess. True humility is not lack of knowledge, money, talents, or any useful abilities but the presence of self-control! Money may be dangerous, but lack of it is even more dangerous! Poor people are tempted to steal, tell lies, cheat, and do many immoral things in order to survive in life.

True humility is easier to see when a person with power exercises self-control. Little power requires little control, and much power requires much control. It does not matter whether the power is money, knowledge, position, or any other thing. Why then should anyone reject the power of money while embracing other forms of power?

Money can defeat poverty

Every loving person on the planet must hate poverty enough to declare a holy war against it. Poverty has led people into crimes and turned many innocent people into victims.

Poverty has broken many promising marriages, killed many dreams, frustrated many desires, and defeated many noble causes. Poverty has brought insult to many respectable people, silenced many important voices, and even forced young children into prostitution in many countries. Many people are having a piece of "hell" here in this world, and many others are on their way to the real Hell because of poverty!

Poverty is bad, and we must do everything within our God-given power to defeat it!

God has blessed us with many weapons, such as wisdom, talent, strategic relationships, education, exposure, and many other powers in our arsenal in order to ensure that we win this holy war. We must build riches in abundance and let money serve our noble causes.

Riches, when properly utilized in combination with other factors, such as proper education, mentorship, hard work, and so on, have the potential to break people free from the hold of material poverty, forever!

Every person with good intentions should plan to be rich! It is okay to show sympathy for those in need and to pray for them to experience the miracle of divine provisions, but it would be far more appreciated if we could also take care of the material needs of such people. It is better to be in a position to give food to those that are hungry than to simply pray for them, trusting God to send them help because we lack the material resources to meet their material needs! God wants you to be His "angel" to those in need. He wants you to be His answer to their prayers and to the prayers that others are saying on their behalf as they dream of coming out of poverty.

Many believers with the hearts to help others do not seem to have enough financial resources to do so. Others have far more money than they need but lack the heart and compassion necessary for helping the needy. Something needs to change! The time has come for those with great hearts to have abundant material resources and for those with the material resources to learn compassion and a sense of moral obligation. How else can the world become a better place?

Children die due to malnutrition in one part of the world while others in a different part of the world waste food. There is enough food in the world to satisfy the needs of everyone on the planet, but like many other essential things of life, the world distributes food neither properly nor fairly.

Do you not think that the time has come for those that have the will to make the world a better place to have the financial conditions to make it happen? Do you not think that the time has come for those that have the mandate for transforming our world to have the money to do so? The truth is that these moments are overdue! The time has come for us to appreciate the enormous power of money and for the church to equip true believers with strong, Bible-based principles and teachings for wealth creation.

Money is a strong weapon for fighting against poverty, and those on a mission to empower others must be willing, committed, and determined to get a lot of it! While money alone will not defeat poverty, it can pave the way and work in combination with other resources to do so. With money, we can establish schools and teach valuable skills to help people become self-reliant. With money, we can create job opportunities for those that are less fortunate.

Do not ignore the importance of money

With just a little more time dedicated to thinking, the average person can come up with a long list of things, good and bad, that one can do with money. It is a credible argument to say that many of the people with the proper understanding and appreciation of the power of money are pursuing it at all costs, undermining moral laws. We also know that money is the reason for most of the wars that nations fight today. It is the reason why there is corruption in the governments of many nations. The *love* of money is the reason why there are many victims of crimes in our time. These may all be true.

However, many great people, harnessing the vast power of money, are doing great things as well. Money is the reason why many are living better lives. Money is making it possible for single individuals to provide drinking water to entire villages today. Kind-hearted people are using money to take care of widows, orphans, drug addicts, strangers, the homeless, and many other people in need, thus making the world a better place. Churches are using money to finance missionaries, plant churches, establish Bible schools, and turn people from darkness to light.

Make up your mind to become rich

If you have not yet made the decision to have material riches, then this is the moment to pause for a minute and do so. Make up your mind to overcome poverty and become richer, not just for your sake but also for the purpose of God's plans and for the sake of so many other lives that you can touch in your lifetime—and probably beyond your time. Your wealth does not only have the potential to touch people in this world, it can actually determine how and where many men and women will spend their eternity because you can use money to propagate the Gospel of salvation to the nations of the earth.

God wants you to make more money than you personally need so that you can affect your world for His glory. Why should you settle for less power if you can have more? The Bible speaks about money, and the time has come for us to get the right position of the Bible on the subject!

4

EARTHLY RICHES ARE FOR YOU!

"The blessing of the LORD, it maketh rich, and he addeth no sorrow with it" (Prov. 10:22).

The Bible is clear about the fact that God blesses the righteous person. This means that He appoints and approves such a person to have special favor, to progress, to enjoy divine protection, and to have good fortune.

The opening passage above shows that God designed His blessings to result in riches without adding sorrow with it.

If God wants His children to be rich, then it is good and proper for us to embrace riches. Since it is possible to obtain riches through honest and godly means, and we can use riches to do good things, it is our holy obligation to work towards becoming richer and more effective in life. We cannot claim to be holy if we know the right things to do and habitually refuse to do them. Having material riches for the glory of God is a good thing.

"Therefore to him that knoweth to do good, and doeth it not, to him it is sin" (James 4:17).

Any person that knows poverty by experience can testify to you that it brings sorrow, pain, rejection, an inferiority complex, strong temptations, depression, and many other things that most of us would rather avoid. Riches may have challenges, but it is far better to be rich than to be poor!

God wants those that fear Him and delight in His commandments to experience His blessings to the extent of becoming mighty and powerful on the earth! He wants them to have riches and wealth in their houses, beyond their time, so that their children will also be mighty!

"Praise ye the LORD. Blessed is the man that feareth the LORD, that delighteth greatly in his commandments. His seed shall be mighty upon earth: the generation of the upright shall be blessed. Wealth and riches shall be in his house: and his righteousness endureth for ever" (Ps. 112:1–3).

The Bible shows us that God does not only consider it appropriate to bless His servants with riches but that He actually finds pleasure in their prosperity. Our God personally enjoys seeing us prosper!

"Let them shout for joy, and be glad, that favour my righteous cause: yea, let them say continually, Let the LORD be magnified, which hath pleasure in the prosperity of his servant" (Ps. 35:27).

If you want to live your life to please God, and it pleases Him to see you prosper, then you should choose to prosper! Go ahead and make your Heavenly Father glad by prospering in all areas of your life. Go for everything that He has in store for you, and make use of the riches in your life to carry out His purpose while you are alive.

God wants His people to prosper in all areas

"Beloved, I wish above all things that thou mayest prosper and be in health, even as thy soul prospereth" (3 John 1:2).

Most Christians will agree that God wants His children to prosper. One begins to notice doctrinal differences when a deeper conversation takes place about the specific areas of prosperity that the Bible means.

Many believe only in the spiritual prosperity of the believer. Based on their understanding, they feel that the believer needs to grow in faith, have a deeper and stronger prayer life, live in purity and in the knowledge of God, and so on. However, they exclude material prosperity from their list and contend that material prosperity would expose the believer to too many temptations and must therefore be contrary to the plan of God for the believer. They forget that poverty also leads to temptations.

We naturally have the desire to survive in life, and we have the tendency to do whatever it takes to stay alive. This can attract temptations towards doing wrong things when we live with extreme poverty. The fact is that both poverty and riches have their temptations.

The psalmist was aware of this fact when he prayed...

"Remove far from me vanity and lies: give me neither poverty nor riches; feed me with food convenient for me: Lest I be full, and deny thee, and say, Who is the LORD? or lest I be poor, and steal, and take the name of my God in vain" (Prov. 30:8–9).

Conscious of the temptations associated with both riches and poverty, Agur, the son of Jake, made the above prayer and asked God simply for the very basic needs of life. While such a prayer is good for personal purity and righteous living, his view did not take into account the need to be rich for reasons beyond personal needs, such as the desire to fulfill divine mandates by touching other lives, prospering God's Kingdom, and leaving an inheritance for generations to come. In any case, the passage goes to show that both the rich and the poor are prone to temptations.

On the other hand, there are those that emphasize the material prosperity of believers, making it their core doctrine and making others accuse them of paying too little attention to other teachings of the Scriptures, such as spiritual development, holiness, sacrifices, and so on. As a result, many of their followers pursue riches just for the sake of riches and for purely selfish motives. Consequently, such followers become rich at the expense of purity, and they end up falling into many temptations, giving Christianity and the biblical teaching on the subject of material prosperity a bad reputation.

The truth is that God wants us to prosper in all areas of our lives. He wants us to be in both spiritual and physical health, as we have read earlier in 3 John 1:2, and to have material riches, as we have seen in Psalm 112:1–3.

The Bible teaches us that God cares about all aspects of our lives and does not want His children to lack any good thing:

"For the LORD God is a sun and shield: the LORD will give grace and glory: no good thing will he withhold from them that walk uprightly. O LORD of hosts, blessed is the man that trusteth in thee" (Ps. 84:11–12).

"And the LORD shall make thee plenteous in goods, in the fruit of thy body, and in the fruit of thy cattle, and in the fruit of thy ground, in the land which the LORD sware unto thy fathers to give thee" (Deut. 28:11).

The Bible presents the righteous as one that has enough to spare and to lend to others:

"Though he fall, he shall not be utterly cast down: for the LORD upholdeth him with his hand. I have been young, and now am old; yet have I not seen the righteous forsaken, nor his seed begging bread. He is ever merciful, and lendeth; and his seed is blessed" (Ps. 37:24–26).

"A good man sheweth favour, and lendeth: he will guide his affairs with discretion" (Ps. 112:5).

To lend to others, one must have. To lend to several people, one must have enough for that many people. God wants His children to be in the position to give to many people.

God's blessed people have always had material riches!

A careful study of both the Old and the New Testament of the Bible will attest to the fact that God has always blessed His children with material riches in addition to the spiritual blessings that they experienced through Him.

Let us see some examples:

a) **Abraham** was very rich.

Many people know Abraham as a friend of God, but they do not realize that he was also very rich, not just spiritually, but in material possessions, such as in cattle, in silver, and in gold!

"And Abram went up out of Egypt, he, and his wife, and all that he had, and Lot with him, into the south. And Abram was very rich in cattle, in silver, and in gold" (Gen. 13:1–2).

b) **Isaac** was rich.

"Then Isaac sowed in that land, and received in the same year an hundredfold: and the LORD blessed him. And the man waxed great, and went forward, and grew until he became very great: For he had possession of flocks, and possession of herds, and great store of servants: and the Philistines envied him" (Gen. 26:12–14).

The Lord blessed Isaac, and as a result, the Bible tells us that he became great, went forward, and became *very great*! His wealth was so much that the Philistines envied him!

At some point, the king became scared of Isaac's increasing

greatness and felt compelled to send him away from the land because he had enough riches to become a threat to the country.

"And Abimelech said unto Isaac, Go from us; for thou art much mightier than we" (Gen. 26:16).

For a king to feel threatened by a single man and to confess that Isaac was mightier than the people of the land were, we can safely conclude that Isaac had noticeable riches.

c) Jacob and Esau were also rich.

Most Bible students know that Jacob received the blessings originally intended for Esau. To protect him from the anger of his brother, his mother sent him away to a far place to live with a family member named Laban. The story is in Genesis chapter twenty-seven. Although Esau missed the double portion of blessing reserved for the first son, he eventually received the leftovers of the blessing of Isaac, their father (Gen. 27:31–41). Nevertheless, make no mistake! The leftover was still enough to make Esau a rich man, as we are about to see.

After several years of separation, these twin brothers finally met and reconciled. Their love for each other after their reconciliation was so strong that they then decided to stay together in the same land. However, they could not stay together for too long, because they were too rich!

"And Esau took his wives, and his sons, and his daughters, and all the persons of his house, and his cattle, and all his beasts, and all his substance, which he had got in the land of Canaan; and went into the country from the face of his brother Jacob. For their riches were more than that they might dwell together; and the land wherein they

were strangers could not bear them because of their cattle" (Gen. 36:6–7).

They had to separate in order to have more room for growth. Otherwise, they ran the risk of misunderstanding and conflicts. Their story goes on to illustrate the fact that material riches go hand-in-hand with God's blessings on the life of a person.

d) The **children of Israel** prospered in Egypt.

"And the children of Israel were fruitful, and increased abundantly, and multiplied, and waxed exceeding mighty; and the land was filled with them" (Ex. 1:7).

They increased in numbers, and their cattle multiplied greatly in the land. The Bible describes them as *"....exceeding mighty."* The king of Egypt rightly observed that *"the children of Israel are more and mightier than we..."* (Exod. 1:9).

Out of fear of having the land taken over by these strangers, the king decided to take preventive measures. As a result, he enslaved the children of Israel and gave orders to kill their male children.

The slavery lasted for over four hundred years, and they lived in poverty during that period. However, by the time the Lord sent Moses to lead them out of the country, He insisted that they left with riches in the form of cattle, fabrics, silver, and gold for all of the years of hard work as part of His blessings. He did not allow them to leave that country empty-handed (Ex. 3:21–22, Ex. 11:2–3, Ex. 12:35–36)! Having material riches had always been part of God's package of blessings for His children.

As the children of Israel prepared to enter the Promised Land, God assured them that they would increase in silver and gold, build houses, plant vineyards, and eat their fill. The material prosperity ahead of them was so much that Moses found it necessary to warn them against taking the credit for their success (Deut. 8:1–17).

He taught them the importance of remembering the secret behind their wealth:

"But thou shalt remember the LORD thy God: for it is he that giveth thee power to get wealth, that he may establish his covenant which he sware unto thy fathers, as it is this day" (Deut. 8:18).

God gives His children power to get wealth because He wants them to be rich. He wants them to be rich because He wants to establish His covenant with them. We shall take a closer look at the significance and importance of this covenant later on in this book.

e) Job was a rich man.

"There was a man in the land of Uz, whose name was Job; and that man was perfect and upright, and one that feared God, and eschewed evil. And there were born unto him seven sons and three daughters. His substance also was seven thousand sheep, and three thousand camels, and five hundred yoke of oxen, and five hundred she asses, and a very great household; so that this man was the greatest of all the men of the east" (Job 1:1–3).

Here we see that Job was *"the greatest of all the men of the east,"* feared God, and served Him with a perfect heart. This man was highly blessed with material riches in addition to his spiritual prosperity. There is no contradiction between material riches and purity. The life of Job is one of many examples testifying to this fact. God's grace does not need poverty to help us live in purity.

f) Even **Obededom** experienced the blessing!

Most students of the Bible will agree that the Ark of the Covenant represented God's presence in the Old Testament. This presence brought victories, divine blessings, and material prosperity. Although a stranger in the land, Obededom experienced these material riches firsthand!

Here is how he experienced the blessings:

As King David and the people transported the Ark, they passed through a gallop, shaking the cart, and it appeared as if the ark was about to fall. One of the young men, a Levite named Uzza, touched it with the intention to prevent it from falling, and he died instantly because he was not supposed to touch the Ark with his hands, even though he may have done so with good intentions (1 Chron. 13:1–12, Num. 4:15). God's presence brings blessings but also requires us to behave ourselves and to line up our lives and actions with His principles. He expects us to follow His instructions at all times and under all circumstances.

The death of Uzza was a very painful and sad experience for David. Afraid of making any more mistakes in handling the ark and thereby invoking God's anger, the king decided to keep a distance from the Ark. He took it to the house of a man called Obededom, a Gittite, one of the strangers living in the land.

Driven by fear, David stayed away from the Ark. Moreover, since he did not want to put any Israelite in danger, he felt that the house of the stranger was the proper place for this now "dangerous" and life-threatening object. The king did not realize at the time that he was doing Obededom a favor and denying himself some special blessings.

In just three months of having the Ark in the house of this stranger, the prosperity of Obededom became the talk of town, and it did not take long before the news reached the king:

"So David would not remove the ark of the LORD unto him into the city of David: but David carried it aside into the house of Obededom the Gittite. And the ark of the LORD continued in the house of Obededom the Gittite three months: and the LORD blessed Obededom, and all his household. And it was told king David, saying, The LORD hath blessed the house of Obededom, and all that pertaineth unto him, because of the ark of God. So David went and brought up the ark of God from the house of Obededom into the city of David with gladness" (2 Sam. 6:10–12).

Notice that this man experienced blessings in *"all that partaineth unto him."* This goes to show one more time that God cares about all aspects of our lives! Material riches are part of God's portion for you when He is on your side.

g) David was rich.

Although David began as a simple young shepherd, he eventually became a very wealthy man. As you are about to read, he had enough riches to personally make gold and silver available for Solomon to begin working on the temple.

"Furthermore David the king said unto all the congregation, Solomon my son, whom alone God hath chosen, is yet young and tender, and the work is great: for the palace is not for man, but for

the LORD God. Now I have prepared with all my might for the house of my God the gold for things to be made of gold, and the silver for things of silver, and the brass for things of brass, the iron for things of iron, and wood for things of wood; onyx stones, and stones to be set, glistering stones, and of divers colors, and all manner of precious stones, and marble stones in abundance. Moreover, because I have set my affection to the house of my God, I have of mine own proper good, of gold and silver, which I have given to the house of my God, over and above all that I have prepared for the holy house, Even three thousand talents of gold, of the gold of Ophir, and seven thousand talents of refined silver, to overlay the walls of the houses withal: The gold for things of gold, and the silver for things of silver, and for all manner of work to be made by the hands of artificers. And who then is willing to consecrate his service this day unto the LORD?" (1 Chron. 29:1–5)

Notice the phrase *" I have of mine own proper good."* In other words, David gave out of his personal wealth. He feared God, and the Lord blessed him with all kinds of blessings, including material riches. God wants you to have material riches beyond measure!

h) Solomon was rich.

The Lord blessed Solomon with wisdom, and people traveled from different parts of the world to go and hear him. Most of them went to him with gifts. Solomon became a very rich king despite the fact that he did not even ask God for riches.

"Now the weight of gold that came to Solomon in one year was six hundred threescore and six talents of gold, Beside that he had of the merchantmen, and of the traffick of the spice merchants, and of all the kings of Arabia, and of the governors of the country. And king

Solomon made two hundred targets of beaten gold: six hundred shekels of gold went to one target. And he made three hundred shields of beaten gold; three pound of gold went to one shield: and the king put them in the house of the forest of Lebanon. Moreover the king made a great throne of ivory, and overlaid it with the best gold. The throne had six steps, and the top of the throne was round behind: and there were stays on either side on the place of the seat, and two lions stood beside the stays. And twelve lions stood there on the one side and on the other upon the six steps: there was not the like made in any kingdom. And all king Solomon's drinking vessels were of gold, and all the vessels of the house of the forest of Lebanon were of pure gold; none were of silver: it was nothing accounted of in the days of Solomon. For the king had at sea a navy of Tharshish with the navy of Hiram: once in three years came the navy of Tharshish, bringing gold, and silver, ivory, and apes, and peacocks. So king Solomon exceeded all the kings of the earth for riches and for wisdom. And all the earth sought to Solomon, to hear his wisdom, which God had put in his heart. And they brought every man his present, vessels of silver, and vessels of gold, and garments, and armor, and spices, horses, and mules, a rate year by year" (1Ki 10:14-25).

Here is a rough calculation to help us put his wealth into perspective. One talent of gold is around thirty kilograms of gold. The passage above shows that he got *"six hundred threescore and six talents"* of gold yearly. One score is twenty. This means that he received about six hundred sixty-six talents of gold yearly. That would be 19,980 kg of gold annually.

At the time of this calculation, a website presented the value of 1 kg of gold as U.S. $58,100. If that is correct and we have to translate Solomon's annual gold income into today's time by simply multiplying his quantity of gold by the market price today, that would be 19,980 kg times $58,100, a stunning total of $1,160,838,000!

Bear in mind that this does not include what he received from the merchants, the spice merchants, numerous kings, and governors. The calculation does not include ivory, silver, peacocks, special wood, and the entire fleet of merchandise that his Navy brought in regularly.

Let us remember that Solomon did not ask for material riches. He asked for knowledge and wisdom in order to be able to rule the people in the right way. Yet God lavished him with abundant material blessings. His heart was set to please God, and God had pleasure in giving him material riches as well, making him the richest king in history.

Here is the proof that Solomon did not ask for material riches:

"In that night did God appear unto Solomon, and said unto him, Ask what I shall give thee. And Solomon said unto God, Thou hast shewed great mercy unto David my father, and hast made me to reign in his stead. Now, O LORD God, let thy promise unto David my father be established: for thou hast made me king over a people like the dust of the earth in multitude. Give me now wisdom and knowledge, that I may go out and come in before this people: for who can judge this thy people, that is so great? And God said to Solomon, Because this was in thine heart, and thou hast not asked riches, wealth, or honour, nor the life of thine enemies, neither yet hast asked long life; but hast asked wisdom and knowledge for thyself, that thou mayest judge my people, over whom I have made thee king: Wisdom and knowledge is granted unto thee; and I will give thee riches, and wealth, and honour, such as none of the kings have had that have been before thee, neither shall there any after thee have the like" (2 Chron. 1:7–12).

Many Bible scholars and opponents of material riches have contended that Solomon's riches were responsible for his downfall and point to his life as an example of how riches can endanger our relationship with God. However, such a suggestion is not reliable because there is no biblical basis for it. Further, the Bible is clear and specific about the cause of Solomon's fall, making it unnecessary for anyone to guess or to speculate on the matter. The Bible does not present material riches as the reason for his failure. We simply need to take God's word as it is.

What does the Bible present as the reason for the fall of King Solomon? Let us read...

"But king Solomon loved many strange women, together with the daughter of Pharaoh, women of the Moabites, Ammonites, Edomites, Zidonians, and Hittites; Of the nations concerning which the LORD said unto the children of Israel, Ye shall not go in to them, neither shall they come in unto you: for surely they will turn away your heart after their gods: Solomon clave unto these in love. And he had seven hundred wives, princesses, and three hundred concubines: and his wives turned away his heart" (1 Kings 11:1–3).

Solomon fell because of his love for strange women. He disregarded God's warning against joining with such women and married several of them for the sake of *"love."* They eventually turned his heart away from God. The king had a serious weakness for beautiful and attractive women, and that became a problem between him and God. Solomon married idolaters, and he allowed these women to turn his heart away from God.

As you can see, he did not fall because of riches. The fact is that the absence of material riches could not have spared him of his fall. Therefore, we cannot blame material riches for the king's mistakes.

Poverty does not guarantee success in anyone's ability to resist sexual temptations. A poor man may have weaknesses for attractive women as well. The only difference between a poor man and Solomon might be that the poor person is less likely to have access to princesses from different nations. Notwithstanding, he will be able to have access to women from poorer neighborhoods and still get in trouble with God in just the same way. Poverty and mediocrity do not protect people from lust and sexual immoralities.

There is no record to show that rich people fall into sexual sins more easily than poor people do. Job was rich and was able to resist sexual temptations. He followed a simple principle and stayed clean.

What principle was it? Here is what he said during his long self-examination:

"I made a covenant with mine eyes; why then should I think upon a maid?" (Job 31:1).

Although he lived in the Old Testament, he understood the secret of staying away from sexual immorality. The Lord Jesus presented the same secret in the New Testament while encouraging people to live free of sexual sins:

"Ye have heard that it was said by them of old time, Thou shalt not commit adultery: But I say unto you, That whosoever looketh on a woman to lust after her hath committed adultery with her already in his heart" (Matt. 5:27–28).

God wants you to have material riches and possess your possessions in purity. Rejoice because it is possible to have material prosperity and live in purity!

i) King Jehoshaphat was rich.

"And the LORD was with Jehoshaphat, because he walked in the first ways of his father David, and sought not unto Baalim; But sought to the LORD God of his father, and walked in his commandments, and not after the doings of Israel. Therefore the LORD stablished the kingdom in his hand; and all Judah brought to Jehoshaphat presents; and he had riches and honour in abundance" (2 Chron. 17:3–5).

Jehoshaphat, the king, *"sought to the LORD God of his father, and walked in his commandments,"* as you can read from the passage above. In addition, *"he had riches and honor in abundance."* Here again we can see godliness and material riches going together. It is not a matter of choosing one or the other. The good news is that we can have both!

j) The **Lord Jesus** also promised material reward for commitment:

"Then Peter began to say unto him, Lo, we have left all, and have followed thee. And Jesus answered and said, Verily I say unto you, There is no man that hath left house, or brethren, or sisters, or father, or mother, or wife, or children, or lands, for my sake, and the gospel's, But he shall receive an hundredfold now in this time, houses, and brethren, and sisters, and mothers, and children, and lands, with persecutions; and in the world to come eternal life" (Mark 10:28–30).

As Peter pointed out their consecration and sacrifice, the Lord assured him that those making such commitments will receive a hundred fold *"now in this time,"* meaning not just in Heaven when they die but also in this present life here on earth! Notice also that the Lord mentioned material blessings such as *houses* and *lands* in addition to eternal life.

We can see clearly that God kept His desire to bless His people with material riches in the New Testament as He did in the Old Testament.

Some may contend that the passage shows persecution as going together with such blessings. However, that is irrelevant because persecution is the result of opposition to a person's stand for God. This opposition can come from people of flawed character that are influenced by spiritual forces because of their fear, jealousy, and suspicion of the believer. However, persecution does not only come to rich believers. Poor believers also suffer persecution. Therefore, as we have seen repeatedly so far, we can conclude that there is nothing wrong with material riches.

k) Believers in the **Early Church** had material riches.

Many Christians are unaware of the fact that people had riches in the Early Church. The church provided for the materials needs of poor people in their time, including widows. Some readers may remember a period when the Apostles needed help in organizing the daily ministration to the widows because some of those in need did not get their share of supplies due to poor coordination:

"And in those days, when the number of the disciples was multiplied,

there arose a murmuring of the Grecians against the Hebrews, because their widows were neglected in the daily ministration" (Acts 6:1).

Many of the believers owned houses and sold them willingly when it was extremely necessary in order to save lives in a time of great famine:

"And with great power gave the apostles witness of the resurrection of the Lord Jesus: and great grace was upon them all. Neither was there any among them that lacked: for as many as were possessors of lands or houses sold them, and brought the prices of the things that were sold, And laid them down at the apostles' feet: and distribution was made unto every man according as he had need. And Joses, who by the apostles was surnamed Barnabas, (which is, being interpreted, The son of consolation,) a Levite, and of the country of Cyprus, Having land, sold it, and brought the money, and laid it at the apostles' feet" (Acts 4:33–37).

Believers had gold, silver, and precious fabrics. Apostle Paul revealed this when he spoke to the church of Ephesus, reminding them that he did not covet the gold of the people when he served them:

"I have coveted no man's silver, or gold, or apparel. Yea, ye yourselves know, that these hands have ministered unto my necessities, and to them that were with me. I have shewed you all things, how that so labouring ye ought to support the weak, and to remember the words of the Lord Jesus, how he said, It is more blessed to give than to receive" (Acts 20:33–35).

Believers also conducted businesses. Aquila and Pricilla were tentmakers, just like Paul. As some readers may know, Paul made

77

and sold tents to generate money for taking care of himself and those around him whenever he had the opportunity to do so (see Acts 20:34–35, 1 Cor. 4:12, 1 Tim. 2:9).

"After these things Paul departed from Athens, and came to Corinth; And found a certain Jew named Aquila, born in Pontus, lately come from Italy, with his wife Priscilla; (because that Claudius had commanded all Jews to depart from Rome:) and came unto them. And because he was of the same craft, he abode with them, and wrought: for by their occupation they were tentmakers" (Act 18:1–3).

There were rich believers in the church under Timothy's care prompting Paul to let Timothy instruct them about how to behave themselves:

"Charge them that are rich in this world, that they be not highminded, nor trust in uncertain riches, but in the living God, who giveth us richly all things to enjoy; That they do good, that they be rich in good works, ready to distribute, willing to communicate; Laying up in store for themselves a good foundation against the time to come, that they may lay hold on eternal life" (1 Tim. 6:17–19).

Many of them had great households and employees, making it necessary for Paul to instruct them about employer and employee working relationships:

"Masters, give unto your servants that which is just and equal; knowing that ye also have a Master in heaven" (Col. 4:1).

"Servants, obey in all things your masters according to the flesh; not with eyeservice, as menpleasers; but in singleness of heart, fearing God: And whatsoever ye do, do it heartily, as to the Lord, and not

unto men; Knowing that of the Lord ye shall receive the reward of the inheritance: for ye serve the Lord Christ. But he that doeth wrong shall receive for the wrong which he hath done: and there is no respect of persons" (Col. 3:22–25).

l) **Paul** also experienced times of abundance.

Most of us know Paul the apostle as a man of great commitment and we are aware of his sacrifices for the Kingdom, but we often forget that his life was not just full of trials, persecutions, and times of lack. He also had times of material abundance while serving in the ministry.

Paul wrote:

"I know both how to be abased, and I know how to abound: every where and in all things I am instructed both to be full and to be hungry, both to abound and to suffer need" (Phil. 4:12).

He understood, by experience, how to be in abundance. In other words, he also had times of abundance.

Paul understood the importance of having material resources beyond one's own needs and actually made sufficient money to take care of himself, and those in need, when his location gave him the opportunity to do so. He was a tentmaker by craft (Acts 18:1-3). As a matter of principle, Paul the Apostle believed in the greater blessing of giving rather than simply receiving.

"Yea, ye yourselves know, that these hands have ministered unto my necessities, and to them that were with me. I have shewed you all things, how that so labouring ye ought to support the weak, and to remember the words of the Lord Jesus, how he said, It is more blessed

to give than to receive" (Acts 20:34–35).

Five reasons why God wants you to have earthly, material riches

There are five main reasons why God wants you and the rest of His children to have material or earthly riches. Here they are, in no particular order of importance or preference:

1. God wants you to represent Him (2 Cor. 5:20).
2. God wants you to enjoy riches (1 Tim. 6:17, Ecc. 5:18–19).
3. God wants you to be rich in good works (1 Tim. 6:17–19, Heb. 13:16, Gal. 6:10).
4. God wants you to leave inheritance for generations (Psalm 13:22).
5. God wants you to prosper His Kingdom (Matt. 6:33, 2 Chron. 31:20–21, John 4:34).

We shall take the next five chapters to look at them more closely.

5

GOD WANTS YOU TO REPRESENT HIM

"Now then we are ambassadors for Christ, as though God did beseech you by us: we pray you in Christ's stead, be ye reconciled to God" (2 Cor. 5:20).

God wants you to represent Him! Have you ever seen yourself as an Ambassador? Well, you had better begin to do so because the opening passage above says that you are one.

We have seen earlier in this book that we must never encourage poverty. We have also seen some of the reasons why people are poor. We have examined the power of money and the fact that God wants His children to have material or earthly riches.

We shall use this chapter and the next four chapters to look at the various reasons why God wants you and every true believer to have material riches. In this chapter, we will be looking at the first reason; namely, that you represent Him here in this world, serving as His ambassador.

An ambassador is an official of the highest rank, sent to a foreign country to serve as a resident representative of the sending state. This person carries the reputation, vision, wishes, values, image, and authority of the sending state, with clear mandates to follow and missions to accomplish.

Ambassadors usually have strict codes of conduct, rules of engagement, and specific instructions about how to represent their countries. They have guidelines about how to dress, what kind of cars to drive, when and how to speak to the media, how to conduct themselves in public, how to relate to the authorities of foreign nations, and much more.

As distinguished diplomats, ambassadors are expected to conduct themselves in the highest possible level of integrity and class; dress in the most appropriate, decent, and respectable fashion; drive in presentable, safe, and reliable cars; live in clean homes in upscale neighborhoods; and have their well-equipped offices in prime locations, with the flags of their nations flying high in clear sight.

Their countries provide them with the budget necessary for them to package their nations properly for credibility and honor. Their nations provide them with financial allowances for clothing, housing, hospitality, and so on. Countries do whatever is appropriate to help their diplomats make positive impressions on their host nations. They know the importance of image.

Take the time to visit the embassies of great nations, and you will see that they strive to display their greatness with enthusiasm, present their cultures with pride, and exhibit the very best of their qualities for every guest to admire. They help to correct misconceptions about their nations and make their lands attractive to travelers for holidays, for cultural research, and for business and investment purposes. Embassies serve as the "face" of their nations, giving the critical first impression that is so important to human perception, as they try to attract people to their countries.

Your world is watching you and judging your God

Like it or not, from the moment that you present yourself to your world as a child of God, you will begin to carry a part of God's reputation with you. You will become an ambassador of God in your environment, and people will judge Christianity by observing your life. If you impress them in good ways, they are likely to have positive views of Christianity.

If you impress them in bad ways, they are likely to have a bad image of Christianity. If you suffer the lack of life's necessities for a prolonged period, they will think that your God does not or cannot take good care of you. If you live in prosperity, they will feel that your relationship with God has something to do with it and will believe that Christianity can make them prosper.

The world will judge God by what they see in your life because you carry God's image and represent Heaven in this world. Your life can attract people to God or repel them from Him, and this can determine how they will spend eternity!

God knows that outward appearance counts in this world

How often have we heard Christians say something like "Well, I am not in this world to please anyone. I am here to serve the Lord, and He knows my heart. How I look on the outside does not matter. I just need to be clean on the inside."

This approach to life is their way of saying that they do not really care about how people see them as long as they have clean hearts and please the Lord in their inward parts. They claim that the outside is not important and that it does not really matter how they appear in the eyes of the world around them as long as they have a healthy inner relationship with God.

To support their position, they would quote from the Bible passage that says:

"But the LORD said unto Samuel, Look not on his countenance, or on the height of his stature; because I have refused him: for the LORD seeth not as man seeth; for man looketh on the outward appearance, but the LORD looketh on the heart" (1 Sam. 16:7).

While they are right in saying that God sees the inward part, they are wrong in undermining the importance of the outward part. The same passage shows that man sees the outward part.

The fact is that God placed us in this world to touch man and to affect lives. If we must reach the world and the world judges by looking at the things that are visible to them on the outside, then how we look on the outside affects how they perceive us and will determine their openness to us and the level of influence that we can have of them.

The passage used here comes from God's instruction to Samuel, the prophet. The Lord sent him to go and anoint one of Jesse's sons to serve as king in Israel in place of King Saul. Samuel, like every other human being, was looking solely on the outside to determine which one of Jesse's sons looked most qualified for the office of a king.

God was compelled to correct the prophet and to let him know that it takes more than outward appearance for one to quality as the Lord's choice for a king. God was telling the prophet that the Lord sees beyond man's outward appearance. This does not in any way mean that the Lord does not see the outside or that the outside is not important. He was saying that the inside is even more important than the outside when it comes to qualifying for God's ordained positions.

Study God's design of the dress of the High Priest in the Old Testament and you will see that God paid special attention to his outward appearance. God wanted him dressed for glory and for beauty. In other words, God wanted the priest to look glorious and to have beautiful garments!

"And thou shalt make holy garments for Aaron thy brother for glory and for beauty" (Ex. 28:2).

That may sound out of place for such a man who was expected to attend to the most holy functions in the Tabernacle, but God was aware of the importance of packaging the priest properly for the sake of the people. Read Exodus 28:1–40, and you will see the detailed description of top quality materials, including gold, precious stones, and fine linen and special attention to embroideries and other design work, especially for a man chosen by God to serve in God's holy office.

Many have argued that God designed Aaron's appearance solely to convey important spiritual messages, but such a narrow position is a weak attempt to exclude the importance of the believer's need for outward beauty, and it denies God's own explanation that clearly states "for glory and for beauty" as part of the reasoning behind the detailed design.

In fact, God went further in the same instruction to point out the importance of dressing the sons serving under Aaron's leadership to have the same glory and outward appeal in their way of dressing.

Look at this:

"And for Aaron's sons thou shalt make coats, and thou shalt make for them girdles, and bonnets shalt thou make for them, for glory and for beauty" (Ex. 28:40)

Notice there again that *"for glory and for beauty"* is part of God's *intention* for the designs.

People respect outward beauty, honor, and external glory

Our world fears the strong, admires the beautiful, respects the rich, appreciates the humanitarian, loves the peacemaker, celebrates the great achiever, and strives to connect with those in high places. Celebrities have influence and command attention wherever they go but not because they are the most intelligent or the most morally upright. On the contrary, many of them are quite immoral. However, these celebrities influence the crowd more than most of the people that are morally upright in our churches today do because most celebrities know how to exhibit the attractive talents, beauties, and qualities of their lives for their audiences to *see*.

People follow and listen to those that they consider successful, powerful, caring, daring, attractive, promising, and appealing. The crowd is sensitive to what they feel, what they see, and how honorable a thing looks to them. The Bible sums up these triggers as *"the lust of the flesh, the lust of the eyes, and the pride of life"* (1 John 2:15–17). Our Creator wired us to care about these areas.

However, the Lord does not want the believer to be subject to the control of such impulses or vanities. We need them to live in this present world, but they must not rule over us. We are to subject all such passions to the word of God and the leading of the Holy Spirit. Notwithstanding, we must recognize their roles in the world and use such knowledge to appeal to those that are controlled by such impulses so that we can influence such people for the glory of God and help them to find true peace with Him.

To get the attention of people, we must pay attention to those things that matter to them. We must pay attention to outward appearance because they matter to man, and we are here on the earth to reach people for God. God encourages us to be appealing to our world and to influence those that are around us by paying attention to the things that matter to them, such as honor, beauty, progress, success, integrity, kindness, and so on.

We live in a world where people look up to those that they consider more successful. They tend to follow people that have reached the things they would love to reach and have been to the places that they would love to go. Our world pays attention to material riches. This is why God wants His children, His

Ambassadors in this world, to be on top, ahead, smarter, more progressive, and more successful, both by the standard of the world and by God's own standard. He wants you to have all that the world dreams of and still serve Him with humility, obeying His voice all of the time, without worshipping any of the material benefits of this world.

Think about these Bible passages:

"Now therefore, if ye will obey my voice indeed, and keep my covenant, then ye shall be a peculiar treasure unto me above all people: for all the earth is mine: And ye shall be unto me a kingdom of priests, and an holy nation. These are the words which thou shalt speak unto the children of Israel" (Ex. 19:5–6).

"For thou art an holy people unto the LORD thy God: the LORD thy God hath chosen thee to be a special people unto himself, above all people that are upon the face of the earth" (Deut. 7:6).

"And the LORD said unto Moses, Take thee Joshua the son of Nun, a man in whom is the spirit, and lay thine hand upon him; And set him before Eleazar the priest, and before all the congregation; and give him a charge in their sight. And thou shalt put some of thine honour upon him, that all the congregation of the children of Israel may be obedient. And he shall stand before Eleazar the priest, who shall ask counsel for him after the judgment of Urim before the LORD: at his word shall they go out, and at his word they shall come in, both he, and all the children of Israel with him, even all the congregation" (Num. 27:18–21).

"And let the beauty of the LORD our God be upon us: and establish thou the work of our hands upon us; yea, the work of our hands establish thou it" (Ps. 90:17).

"Out of Zion, the perfection of beauty, God hath shined" (Ps. 50:2).

"Save now, I beseech thee, O LORD: O LORD, I beseech thee, send now prosperity" (Ps. 118:25).

Are we saying that it is all about the outside? No! That would be wrong. It is about both the inside and the outside. The Lord looks at the inside, and man looks at the outside. We need to be true to God and appealing to man. We need to please God and influence man without compromising our stand with God. God left you here to be fruitful. This requires you to be influential. That is why He wants you to have material riches, wisdom, purity, courage, spiritual power, academic titles, promotions, and everything else that matters to Heaven and to the earth.

Heaven is counting on you to represent God's image properly

Countries strive to take the best possible care of their embassies and ambassadors because they are conscious of the importance of image and reputation. Top companies have strict guidelines for about how they want their agents to represent them. They prescribe strict branding strategies in order to ensure proper representation of their brands. They do these things because they understand the importance of image. They know that they can never succeed beyond their reputations. We must have the importance of reputation in mind as we make efforts to prosper God's Kingdom.

Most people will treat us as they perceive us to be and not as we truly are. Our presentations affect their perception of us, and speak of our God, church, company, nation, race, organization, and all that we represent. Always bear in mind that you represent someone, some people, an idea, an organization, or a nation wherever you go.

If you are a citizen of a country in a foreign land, people are likely to make some conscious or unconscious conclusions about your country by observing your life.

Once they make a conclusion about you, the next time that they see someone from the same country, the picture they have in mind about you will show up, and they will begin to see that person through that picture. This is what leads to prejudice.

People say that the first impression is very important. However, in real life, most people will judge you long before you get the opportunity to make the first impression. They will judge you, not by your own character or first impression but by the first impression of those that represented you long before you came into the picture. We may call this prejudice or profiling, but it is part of the human nature. It does not sound fair, but it is a fact!

In the same way that people judge you because of the behavior of others, they will judge others because of your behavior. Whether you like it or not, your life will represent people that never consciously chose you to represent them. You carry their image with you.

In the same way, you carry the image of God's Kingdom. What people see in you can affect their opinions about God's people and influence their decisions about God, church, the Bible, prayers, Christianity, and so on. This is why you cannot afford to be careless about what they see in you.

What they see in us influences their attitude towards the Gospel message that we present to them. Their attitude towards the Gospel of the Lord Jesus Christ will determine where they spend eternity. Their salvation thus depends, largely, on how they perceive us.

They constantly watch us to see if we live what we preach, if our God is good to us, if we shine as lights in this world, and if we are true examples of those things that appeal to both their internal consciences and outward senses. Material prosperity in this world appeals to the senses of the people in this world—the people that we are alive to reach with the Gospel.

Therefore, every believer has a very serious responsibility to represent God in this world, in all of His attributes, properly. We must live in line with the teachings of the Scriptures. To believe in the Bible and consciously live contrary to it is hypocrisy! Hypocrisy can hinder others from entering into the Kingdom.

Speaking of the adverse effects of hypocrisy, Paul, by divine inspiration, wrote:

"And art confident that thou thyself art a guide of the blind, a light of them which are in darkness, An instructor of the foolish, a teacher of babes, which hast the form of knowledge and of the truth in the law. Thou therefore which teachest another, teachest thou not thyself? thou that preachest a man should not steal, dost thou steal? Thou that sayest a man should not commit adultery, dost thou commit adultery? thou that abhorrest idols, dost thou commit sacrilege? Thou that makest thy boast of the law, through breaking the law dishonorest thou God? For the name of God is blasphemed among the Gentiles through you, as it is written" (Rom. 2:19–24).

The Bible is clear about the fact that the prosperity of God's people brings glory to God, and their failures in any given area cause people to blaspheme God. Here are some of them:

"Now therefore, what have I here, saith the LORD, that my people is taken away for nought? they that rule over them make them to howl, saith the LORD; and my name continually every day is blasphemed" (Is. 52:5).

"All that pass by clap their hands at thee; they hiss and wag their head at the daughter of Jerusalem, saying, Is this the city that men call The perfection of beauty, The joy of the whole earth? All thine enemies have opened their mouth against thee: they hiss and gnash the teeth: they say, We have swallowed her up: certainly this is the day that we looked for; we have found, we have seen it" (Lam. 2:15–16).

"I will therefore that the younger women marry, bear children, guide the house, give none occasion to the adversary to speak reproachfully" (1 Tim. 5:14).

"Ye are the salt of the earth: but if the salt have lost his savour, wherewith shall it be salted? it is thenceforth good for nothing, but to be cast out, and to be trodden under foot of men. Ye are the light of the world. A city that is set on an hill cannot be hid. Neither do men light a candle, and put it under a bushel, but on a candlestick; and it giveth light unto all that are in the house. Let your light so shine before men, that they may see your good works, and glorify your Father which is in heaven" (Matt. 5:13–16).

God goes the extra mile for His name's sake

God delivers His children, protects them, guides them, forgives them, disciplines them, restores them, and does many things with them and through them, not just because of them but because He cares about His own name, image, and reputation among those that do not know Him.

He wants to keep His name honorable so that He can continue to command respect among those that are strangers to His ways. He takes care of His diplomats on the earth so that He can continue to have a great image on the earth. This is part of God's strategy for saving the lost!

<u>Consider these Bible passages:</u>

"And when they entered unto the heathen, whither they went, they profaned my holy name, when they said to them, These are the people of the LORD, and are gone forth out of his land. But I had pity for mine holy name, which the house of Israel had profaned among the heathen, whither they went. Therefore say unto the house of Israel, Thus saith the Lord GOD; I do not this for your sakes, O house of Israel, but for mine holy name's sake, which ye have profaned among the heathen, whither ye went. And I will sanctify my great name, which was profaned among the heathen, which ye have profaned in the midst of them; and the heathen shall know that I am the LORD, saith the Lord GOD, when I shall be sanctified in you before their eyes" (Ezek. 36:20–23).

"And the LORD said unto Moses, Go, get thee down; for thy people, which thou broughtest out of the land of Egypt, have corrupted themselves: They have turned aside quickly out of the way which I commanded them: they have made them a molten calf, and have worshipped it, and have sacrificed thereunto, and said, These be thy

gods, O Israel, which have brought thee up out of the land of Egypt. And the LORD said unto Moses, I have seen this people, and, behold, it is a stiffnecked people: Now therefore let me alone, that my wrath may wax hot against them, and that I may consume them: and I will make of thee a great nation. And Moses besought the LORD his God, and said, LORD, why doth thy wrath wax hot against thy people, which thou hast brought forth out of the land of Egypt with great power, and with a mighty hand? Wherefore should the Egyptians speak, and say, For mischief did he bring them out, to slay them in the mountains, and to consume them from the face of the earth? Turn from thy fierce wrath, and repent of this evil against thy people. Remember Abraham, Isaac, and Israel, thy servants, to whom thou swarest by thine own self, and saidst unto them, I will multiply your seed as the stars of heaven, and all this land that I have spoken of will I give unto your seed, and they shall inherit it for ever. And the LORD repented of the evil which he thought to do unto his people" (Ex. 32:7–14).

"And the LORD said unto Moses, How long will this people provoke me? and how long will it be ere they believe me, for all the signs which I have shewed among them? I will smite them with the pestilence, and disinherit them, and will make of thee a greater nation and mightier than they. And Moses said unto the LORD, Then the Egyptians shall hear it, (for thou broughtest up this people in thy might from among them;) And they will tell it to the inhabitants of this land: for they have heard that thou LORD art among this people, that thou LORD art seen face to face, and that thy cloud standeth over them, and that thou goest before them, by day time in a pillar of a cloud, and in a pillar of fire by night. Now if thou shalt kill all this people as one man, then the nations which have heard the fame of thee will speak, saying, Because the LORD was not able to bring this people into the land which he sware unto them, therefore he hath slain them in the wilderness" (Num. 14:11–16).
"We have sinned with our fathers, we have committed iniquity, we

have done wickedly. Our fathers understood not thy wonders in Egypt; they remembered not the multitude of thy mercies; but provoked him at the sea, even at the Red sea. Nevertheless he saved them for his name's sake, that he might make his mighty power to be known" (Ps. 106:6–8).

We must represent God in His various aspects

Some readers may ask the question "Can we not simply be honest, loving, caring, pure, and strong spiritually and still represent God well?" The answer is simple: All of the great qualities, such as honesty, loving, caring, purity, and so on, are important and necessary, but they are not complete without earthly riches.

As God's representatives in this world, we must be determined to represent God in *every aspect* that He has presented Himself in His word. He is a God of mercy, yet a God of judgment. He is kind-hearted and merciful, yet a consuming fire. He is a God of peace, yet of war. He is a God of freedom, yet a God of order and discipline. He has many sides, and we need to let our world see all of them!

Our God says that we must be humble, yet He wants us to be the head and not the tail, the first, and not the last (Deut. 28:13)! He teaches us to be content, yet He encourages us to prosper in abundance in order to prosper His work, enjoy life, and help those that are in need. He teaches us to be simple, yet He plans to lift us up when we do so (James 4:10). He asks us to do alms in secret (Matt. 6:3), yet demands that we do good works for men to see so that they can glorify Him (Matt. 5:13–16). He wants us to be Heaven-minded, yet He demands that we take territories here on earth and expand His work.

95

Our Lord is the Prince of Peace, yet the Man of War! He is the Lamb of God, yet the Lion of the tribe of Judah! God has many aspects. These attributes are not in conflict. On the contrary, they complement one another depending on the situations, persons, places, seasons, and times.

One of the biggest mistakes Christians have made over the years is that we have selected "favorite" portions of the Bible that tend to appeal to our own backgrounds, preferences, cultures, traditions, ambitions, personalities, and so on, promoting those parts as "more important" and neglecting other parts of the Bible. We tend to forget that every scripture is God's inspiration for our own learning and effectiveness as we live to do God's work in this world.

"All scripture is given by inspiration of God, and is profitable for doctrine, for reproof, for correction, for instruction in righteousness: That the man of God may be perfect, thoroughly furnished unto all good works" (2 Tim. 3:16–17).

The consequence of picking and choosing our "favorite" parts of the Scriptures while ignoring other parts of the word of God is that we end up leaving our world in the dark about the full picture of the God that we serve. For example, some of the people fighting to eradicate poverty from the world today think that Christianity encourages poverty. Many of them have no idea that true Christianity eradicates poverty.

The time has come for us to preach and to model the total Gospel to the total man! God has many sides to many people depending on their circumstances. We have no rights to restrict Him to our own limited and imperfect preferences. We must present Him to the people in need in the same way that His word presents Him to them.

To those that are sick, He is the ultimate Healer. To those that are ignorant, He is the fountain of knowledge. To them that are low, He uplifts. To those that are poor, He makes one rich. To those that are bound, He is the Deliverer. To those that are in darkness, He is the Light of the world. To those that are tired, He will give rest. To those that are on their way to eternal damnation, the Lord Jesus Christ is the Way, the Truth, and the Life, and their opportunity to spend eternity with God. To those that are rich, He has purpose for their riches and a clear pathway to true inner fulfillment.

Our God answers the cry of every heart and meets the deepest secret needs of every person, in every situation, in every part of the world. We must not limit Him to our personal preferences. God wants to reach people through us. Therefore, we must look at life, not just from our perspectives but also from the perspectives of the world that we are in this life to touch. That is what it will take to be effective representatives of God's Kingdom in this world.

How important is God's reputation to you?

God has always paid attention to the outside when trying to reach man. Bible students know that the Tabernacle had beautiful color combinations with a distinct design approach to it. The beauty of the temple of King Solomon attracted tourists from different parts of the world. The Bible describes Heaven in the language of beauty, fashion, and architectural excellence, making the place appealing to the human senses and natural interests.

God does not only speak of Heaven as a place of peace, praise and worship, and perfect health. He also talks of streets of gold, beautiful mansions, water as clear as crystal, and beautiful garments! Why would God pay so much attention to material details if the outside were not important? The fact is that God must speak the language of man and appeal to him in order to reach man successfully! God knows that man pays attentions to the outside and respects material success.

What rights do we then have to do otherwise and to claim that the outside is not important? Do we now profess to know how to reach man better than the God who created man? We must repent! The time has come for us to follow God's example and to use His formula so that we can be more effective.

Since our mission in the world is to reach the world, we must pay attention to the things that matter to the world. Most of the people that we meet will look at us on the outside before paying attention to what we have on the inside.

From the moment that they meet us, they will notice how we look, the clothes we wear, how we behave, the way we speak, how we treat others, and so on. Some will even pay attention to the health status of our teeth and to how we smell! If they like what they see, feel, hear, and smell, then they may consider getting to know us better and may be interested in discovering the "secrets" behind the things that they admire about us.

If we disregard the outside, then we turn people off before they get the opportunity to know us. This will deny them the chance to even consider the Message. Why should you or any believer deny people the chance to discover a true child of God by presenting them the wrong image on the outside? People must have a fair chance to know us before making up their minds about the faith that we represent and the Gospel message that we preach.

Some of the people accused of rejecting the Christian faith did not reject the faith. They actually did not get a real chance to know the faith. The sad truth is that someone claiming to be a Christian misrepresented Christianity to them and gave a wrong image of the Lord Jesus Christ! Such people simply rejected the wrong image presented to them.

Leading companies do not tolerate any misrepresentation of their brands, yet Christians misrepresent the Lord daily. As serious believers, we must care about how the world perceives us.

Like the psalmist in the Bible, we must care about the Lord's reputation. While going through challenges, his greatest concern was not just his difficult condition. The toughest thing for him was the potential impact of his condition on the lives of those in the world around him. He was worried that his enemies were using his situation to question God's faithfulness.

The psalmist knew that he was an ambassador, and he longed for God with a deep desire for a breakthrough as he cried through the night, wishing to put an end to the doubts in the minds of the world around him about his God.

<u>Here is the passage:</u>

"As the hart panteth after the water brooks, so panteth my soul after

99

thee, O God. My soul thirsteth for God, for the living God: when shall I come and appear before God? My tears have been my meat day and night, while they continually say unto me, Where is thy God?" (Ps. 42:1–3).

He could just not stand people asking, *"Where is thy God?"* He did not enjoy hearing people perceive his God as one who abandons His servants. He cared about God's reputation and felt the pain of their words deep within his bones.

"As with a sword in my bones, mine enemies reproach me; while they say daily unto me, Where is thy God?" (Ps. 42:10).

The condition of God's children definitely affects God's reputation in the world. The book of Joel showed the same concern and called on God's people to fast and pray for Him to intervene in the condition of His children in order to stop people from questioning God's faithfulness.

Here is the passage:

"Gather the people, sanctify the congregation, assemble the elders, gather the children, and those that suck the breasts: let the bridegroom go forth of his chamber, and the bride out of her closet. Let the priests, the ministers of the LORD, weep between the porch and the altar, and let them say, Spare thy people, O LORD, and give not thine heritage to reproach, that the heathen should rule over them: wherefore should they say among the people, Where is their God?" (Joel 2:16–17).

Will you embrace God's earthly blessings?

The world pays attention to riches and celebrates material success.

Although simplicity may impress people in the church, the human beings outside of the church hate poverty and love abundance! They appreciate simplicity as well, but not the simplicity of those that they consider poor and unsuccessful in life.

The simplicity of a single rich man out there will get their attention far more than the apparent humility of a hundred poor Christians, even if such Christians have big Bibles, attend every church service, and speak in tongues!

Simplicity is a choice to the rich. To the poor, it is often a forced condition. Therefore, the rich person's simplicity has a greater potential to convey humility to our world than a poor person's simplicity has. To teach the world humility, you must rise to the top and reach out to your world from there. This will give you a larger audience for your message. That is why you must embrace God's will for your earthly riches!

God wants you to have everything that the world dreams of so that the world can see His goodness, riches, grace, generosity, and glory through your life. You must make up your mind to have far more riches than you need in this world without putting your heart or your trust in your possessions. Walk with God to prosper, and remember Him as the secret of your success so that you can live to give Him the honor and the glory due His name.

Even if you do not think that you personally need riches, you still have to be rich because God wants to present His children to the world as blessed in all areas, including the area of material possessions, because the world looks at the outside and pays attention to the lifestyles of God's children. You are an ambassador of Heaven, whether you like it or not! God wants you

101

to represent Him in material riches in just the same way that you represent Him in spiritual riches.

Will you work with Him towards the next level of your earthly material riches? Proceed to the next chapter to read one more of the five reasons why God wants you to have earthly riches.

6

GOD WANTS YOU TO ENJOY MATERIAL BLESSINGS

"Behold that which I have seen: it is good and comely for one to eat and to drink, and to enjoy the good of all his labor that he taketh under the sun all the days of his life, which God giveth him: for it is his portion. Every man also to whom God hath given riches and wealth, and hath given him power to eat thereof, and to take his portion, and to rejoice in his labour; this is the gift of God" (Ecc. 5:18–19).

We saw in the last chapter that God wants you to have material riches in this world because you represent Him and the world will judge you and Him -and all that you represent - by looking at your life. Now we shall see the second reason why God wants you to have material riches in this world; namely, for you to enjoy them!

To enjoy means to experience the benefit of something delightful and pleasurable. It has to do with finding pleasure in the intentions, process, or outcome of a thing, a person, or a place. To enjoy means to be delighted and happy with something that stirs up our passion.

Enjoyment renews our energy, makes us appreciative of the blessings in our lives, and helps us to move beyond the weights associated with hard work and prolonged commitment. Times of enjoyment remind us of God's faithfulness. Those that learn to enjoy the fruits of their labor also have greater drive and renewed energy to work harder.

Enjoyment allows you to experience the reward of your efforts personally. Enjoying our efforts makes us more committed and fruitful for a longer period. God wants you to be fruitful for the rest of your life. Therefore, you must learn to enjoy His blessings and the fruits of your labor.

Enjoyment is part of God's plans for your life

The Bible consistently shows that God wants His children to enjoy His blessings in their lives. If God wants something, then we can safely assume that He has good reasons for it.

The journey towards becoming rich and successful is often full of challenges and intense pressure. It is common to feel drained spiritually and physically along the way. Therefore, it is essential to replenish the spirit, renew the mind, and refresh the body from time to time. While self-denial is also part of the lifestyle of progressive people, we must be careful to avoid *self-neglect*. There is a thin line between self-denial and self-neglect.

Self-denial has to do with the exercise of personal discipline in appropriate level, times, and situations in order to reach higher goals. Self-neglect is a careless, habitual, and often unnecessary neglect of one's personal needs for unprofitable reasons. Many people cross this thin line, engaging in self-neglect and thinking that they are exercising self-denial.

Many people age faster than they should and lose the functions of their vital organs, reducing the number of years of their lives, because their zeal and determination to accomplish greater goals drive them to develop the bad habit of prolonged self-neglect. Do not follow such careless examples.

Paul the Apostle understood the importance of hard work and self-denial (1 Cor. 15:9–10, 2 Cor. 11:23–30), yet he knew the importance of enjoying God's riches as well and found it necessary to include it in his letter to Timothy, as you can read in the following Bible passage:

"Charge them that are rich in this world, that they be not highminded, nor trust in uncertain riches, but in the living God, who giveth us richly all things to enjoy" (1 Ti 6:17).

The passage clearly states that God wants those with riches to enjoy them.

The Lord Jesus did not forget to let His disciples know the importance of enjoying the fruit of their labor when He sent them out to preach. He encouraged them to enjoy good hospitality and to eat and drink whenever they found the opportunity:

"And into whatsoever house ye enter, first say, Peace be to this house. And if the son of peace be there, your peace shall rest upon it: if not, it shall turn to you again. And in the same house remain, eating and drinking such things as they give: for the laborer is worthy of his hire. Go not from house to house. And into whatsoever city ye enter, and

they receive you, eat such things as are set before you" (Luke 10:5–8).

The Lord also taught His disciples to rest when necessary. After sending them out to preach the Gospel on one occasion, they returned with several testimonies. He listened to them gladly and did not hesitate to have them enjoy some quietness and a time of rest. He personally instructed them to go into a quiet location and get some rest.

Here is the passage:

"And the apostles gathered themselves together unto Jesus, and told him all things, both what they had done, and what they had taught. And he said unto them, Come ye yourselves apart into a desert place, and rest a while: for there were many coming and going, and they had no leisure so much as to eat. And they departed into a desert place by ship privately" (Mark 6:30–32).

It is an established principle with God that those laboring, whether they are humans or animals, have to enjoy the fruits of their labor:

"The husbandman that laboureth must be first partaker of the fruits" (2 Tim. 2:6).

"Let the elders that rule well be counted worthy of double honour, especially they who labour in the word and doctrine. For the scripture saith, Thou shalt not muzzle the ox that treadeth out the corn. And, The labourer is worthy of his reward" (1 Tim. 5:17–18).

"Thou shalt not muzzle the ox when he treadeth out the corn" (Deut. 25:4).

"For it is written in the law of Moses, thou shalt not muzzle the mouth of the ox that treadeth out the corn. Doth God take care for oxen? Or saith he it altogether for our sakes? For our sakes, no doubt, this is written: that he that ploweth should plow in hope; and that he that thresheth in hope should be partaker of his hope" (1 Cor. 9:9–10).

Enjoyment is part of God's gift to hardworking people

Many hardworking believers tend to detest enjoyment and feel guilty whenever they have to take some time off from the work of the Kingdom. Consequently, they often look exhausted and worn out because they invest a lot of time on other people and forget the importance of taking good care of themselves and staying fresh and renewed for greater results.

Many pastors, in their zeal to serve the Lord, are guilty of self-neglect because they fail to take care of their own basic needs. They look older than they are and make ministry unattractive to potential successors, thereby threatening the future of the Gospel of the Lord Jesus Christ.

Traveling around the world as a minister of the Gospel brings one in contact with many dedicated pastors and their families. It is common to meet children of pastors that do not dream of serving in the ministry, not just because of the tough life associated with ministry but often more because of the self-neglect of their parents.

The ministry vocation that God intended to be a privilege feels like punishment to them because their parents do not enjoy ministry. These children know first-hand the price that their parents pay daily and the little appreciation that they get from some selfish, unthankful, insatiable, and ever-demanding church members!

Some pastors subject their families to unnecessary pressure because they fear that church members would criticize them if they enjoyed material blessings. There is an unholy expectation in many places that pastors have to suffer in poverty and lack in this world in order for them to serve God's people effectively and make it to Heaven.

The children of these pastors remember vividly when they could not afford to buy new shoes because their parents used the family's money to cover church expenses while other church members could afford luxurious vacations, own several cars, waste food, and burn fireworks celebrating end-of-year events.

It is unfortunate that many of these children pay more than their fair share of the price for the Gospel while so many church members only spend time criticizing them and increasing the pressure on their lives instead of thinking of ways to help them enjoy the work of the Lord.

Many churchgoers are comfortable seeing their pastors in material lack, thinking that such pastors ought to "suffer for Jesus"! These members protest when spiritual leaders get opportunities to enjoy material blessings.

Aware of this mindset in believers, many church leaders make unnecessary sacrifices, subjecting their families to material hardship and often feel "guilty" whenever they have little opportunities to enjoy the good things of this world. They find it difficult to enjoy life when God blesses them with material benefits because they know that God's people do not wish to see them enjoying such things.

These leaders often allow the fear of false accusations and condemnations from church members to spoil their enjoyment long before they begin enjoying the fruits of their labor!

It is unfortunate that we have grown to associate spirituality with poverty and material lack. We think that those that are spiritual should settle for the least of the material provisions in this life, and we expect people to become poorer in material terms as they become more spiritual.

As a result, many Christians seeking their places and rewards in Heaven feel that they have to abandon material blessings in this world and settle for less of the good things of this life in order to become more spiritual. As we have seen earlier in this book, this way of thinking is not only wrong but it is detrimental to the furtherance of the Gospel of the Lord Jesus Christ!

We need to worry about the future of the work of God when we see that many children of the people now active in the ministry have no strong desires to enter into ministry, because of the extraordinary and the often-unnecessary material prices that their parents continue to pay for the work of God. It is sad because ministry is supposed to be a coveted vocation, a privileged profession, and an honorable calling to serve the Almighty God and secure humanity's place in eternity with God.

Anyone that understands God's heart knows that God does not want anyone to serve Him in vain. The Bible consistently shows us that there are always spiritual and material rewards for serving God - in this world and in eternity.

The Bible says:

"Therefore, my beloved brethren, be ye stedfast, unmoveable, always abounding in the work of the Lord, forasmuch as ye know that your labour is not in vain in the Lord" (1 Cor. 15:58).

"Be ye strong therefore, and let not your hands be weak: for your work shall be rewarded" (2 Chron. 15:7).

"And the LORD said unto Satan, Hast thou considered my servant Job, that there is none like him in the earth, a perfect and an upright man, one that feareth God, and escheweth evil? Then Satan answered the LORD, and said, Doth Job fear God for nought? Hast not thou made an hedge about him, and about his house, and about all that he hath on every side? thou hast blessed the work of his hands, and his substance is increased in the land" (Job 1:8–10).

"After these things the word of the LORD came unto Abram in a vision, saying, Fear not, Abram: I am thy shield, and thy exceeding great reward. And Abram said, LORD God, what wilt thou give me, seeing I go childless, and the steward of my house is this Eliezer of Damascus? And Abram said, Behold, to me thou hast given no seed: and, lo, one born in my house is mine heir. And, behold, the word of the LORD came unto him, saying, This shall not be thine heir; but he that shall come forth out of thine own bowels shall be thine heir. And he brought him forth abroad, and said, Look now toward heaven, and tell the stars, if thou be able to number them: and he said unto him, So shall thy seed be. And he believed in the LORD; and he counted it to him for righteousness. And he said unto him, I am the LORD that brought thee out of Ur of the Chaldees, to give thee this land to inherit it" (Gen. 15:1–7).

"So the LORD blessed the latter end of Job more than his beginning: for he had fourteen thousand sheep, and six thousand camels, and a thousand yoke of oxen, and a thousand she asses" (Job 42:12).

"But without faith it is impossible to please him: for he that cometh to God must believe that he is, and that he is a rewarder of them that diligently seek him" (Heb. 11:6).

God has many ways of rewarding those that seek Him, follow Him, and work hard. Giving them opportunities to enjoy life is part of His gift to them:

"For what hath man of all his labour, and of the vexation of his heart, wherein he hath laboured under the sun? For all his days are sorrows, and his travail grief; yea, his heart taketh not rest in the night. This is also vanity. There is nothing better for a man, than that he should eat and drink, and that he should make his soul enjoy good in his labour. This also I saw, that it was from the hand of God" (Ecc. 2:22–24).

"And also that every man should eat and drink, and enjoy the good of all his labour, it is the gift of God" (Ecc. 3:13).

If you build a house, God wants you to enjoy it! If you plant a vineyard, He wants you to eat the fruits. If you are married, He wants you to enjoy your marriage. If you train people, He wants you to find true fulfillment by watching them grow and enjoying their appreciation. If you have children, He wants you to enjoy them.

Learn to enjoy your portion of God's blessings to the full! Ignorant people may criticize you for this, but you must never apologize for enjoying the blessings of God in your life. It is His will for you to have and to enjoy earthly riches! Why should you refuse anything that is part of God's will for your life?

The word of God says:

"Blessed is every one that feareth the LORD; that walketh in his ways. For thou shalt eat the labour of thine hands: happy shalt thou be, and it shall be well with thee. Thy wife shall be as a fruitful vine by the sides of thine house: thy children like olive plants round about thy table. Behold, that thus shall the man be blessed that feareth the LORD" (Ps. 128:1–4).

"Drink waters out of thine own cistern, and running waters out of thine own well. Let thy fountains be dispersed abroad, and rivers of waters in the streets. Let them be only thine own, and not strangers' with thee. Let thy fountain be blessed: and rejoice with the wife of thy youth. Let her be as the loving hind and pleasant roe; let her breasts satisfy thee at all times; and be thou ravished always with her love. And why wilt thou, my son, be ravished with a strange woman, and embrace the bosom of a stranger?" (Prov. 5:15–20).

"Live joyfully with the wife whom thou lovest all the days of the life of thy vanity, which he hath given thee under the sun, all the days of thy vanity: for that is thy portion in this life, and in thy labour which thou takest under the sun" (Ecc. 9:9).

"And it came to pass, when he had been there a long time, that Abimelech king of the Philistines looked out at a window, and saw, and, behold, Isaac was sporting with Rebekah his wife" (Gen. 26:8).

"For as a young man marrieth a virgin, so shall thy sons marry thee: and as the bridegroom rejoiceth over the bride, so shall thy God rejoice over thee" (Is. 62:5).

112

"Rid me, and deliver me from the hand of strange children, whose mouth speaketh vanity, and their right hand is a right hand of falsehood: That our sons may be as plants grown up in their youth; that our daughters may be as corner stones, polished after the similitude of a palace: That our garners may be full, affording all manner of store: that our sheep may bring forth thousands and ten thousands in our streets: That our oxen may be strong to labour; that there be no breaking in, nor going out; that there be no complaining in our streets. Happy is that people, that is in such a case: yea, happy is that people, whose God is the LORD" (Ps. 144:11–15).

"And they shall build houses, and inhabit them; and they shall plant vineyards, and eat the fruit of them. They shall not build, and another inhabit; they shall not plant, and another eat: for as the days of a tree are the days of my people, and mine elect shall long enjoy the work of their hands. They shall not labour in vain, nor bring forth for trouble; for they are the seed of the blessed of the LORD, and their offspring with them. And it shall come to pass, that before they call, I will answer; and while they are yet speaking, I will hear" (Is. 65:21–24).

It is wrong for the righteous to labor and not enjoy the fruits

It is contrary to the will of God for a blessed person to labor and not partake in the benefits. Actually, the Bible considers it punishment, and even a curse, for a person to work hard and not enjoy the fruits. That is a lifestyle reserved for people living contrary to the will of God!

Speaking to those living in disobedience, the Lord says:

"And if ye shall despise my statutes, or if your soul abhor my judgments, so that ye will not do all my commandments, but that ye break my covenant: I also will do this unto you; I will even appoint over you terror, consumption, and the burning ague, that shall consume the eyes, and cause sorrow of heart: and ye shall sow your seed in vain, for your enemies shall eat it" (Lev. 26:15–16).

"Thou shalt betroth a wife, and another man shall lie with her: thou shalt build an house, and thou shalt not dwell therein: thou shalt plant a vineyard, and shalt not gather the grapes thereof. Thine ox shall be slain before thine eyes, and thou shalt not eat thereof: thine ass shall be violently taken away from before thy face, and shall not be restored to thee: thy sheep shall be given unto thine enemies, and thou shalt have none to rescue them. Thy sons and thy daughters shall be given unto another people, and thine eyes shall look, and fail with longing for them all the day long: and there shall be no might in thine hand. The fruit of thy land, and all thy labours, shall a nation which thou knowest not eat up; and thou shalt be only oppressed and crushed alway: So that thou shalt be mad for the sight of thine eyes which thou shalt see" (Deut. 28:30–34).

"Remember, O LORD, what is come upon us: consider, and behold our reproach. Our inheritance is turned to strangers, our houses to aliens" (Lam. 5:1–2).

The above passages shall not be your portion, from now onwards, in Jesus' name! God wants you to enjoy material riches.

Enjoyment was even a mandate to God's soldiers

Enjoying one's blessings is so important to God that He made it mandatory for soldiers in the Old Testament to enjoy their blessings before going to war.

Read His pre-battle instructions to the children of Israel and understand for yourself:

"When thou goest out to battle against thine enemies, and seest horses, and chariots, and a people more than thou, be not afraid of them: for the LORD thy God is with thee, which brought thee up out of the land of Egypt. And it shall be, when ye are come nigh unto the battle, that the priest shall approach and speak unto the people, And shall say unto them, Hear, O Israel, ye approach this day unto battle against your enemies: let not your hearts faint, fear not, and do not tremble, neither be ye terrified because of them; For the LORD your God is he that goeth with you, to fight for you against your enemies, to save you. And the officers shall speak unto the people, saying, What man is there that hath built a new house, and hath not dedicated it? let him go and return to his house, lest he die in the battle, and another man dedicate it. And what man is he that hath planted a vineyard, and hath not yet eaten of it? let him also go and return unto his house, lest he die in the battle, and another man eat of it. And what man is there that hath betrothed a wife, and hath not taken her? let him go and return unto his house, lest he die in the battle, and another man take her" (Deut. 20:1–7).

Make up your mind to enjoy the blessings of God, and do not make a secret of God's goodness in your life. To those that know you, your lifestyle will speak more of the God that you serve than your words will ever be able to tell.

Therefore, let your life speak as the world around you sees

your progress in God. Eat healthy, live comfortably, dress presentably, increase in knowledge, and excel in everything that you do. Your life carries God's reputation, and your world is watching you!

Know your "portion" as a faithful steward

If you live faithfully with God and follow His principles for material prosperity, you will get to a place of abundance and watch riches come to you from different directions. While God wants you to enjoy your life and to be a great testimony of His goodness, the fact that money arrived through your bank account on your name in the form of salaries, dividends, commission, or profit after your hard work and legitimate business effort does not automatically mean that God wants the money to serve you alone. He may intend for a part of that money to serve others.

To please God, you must learn to know the mission of His money in your life. Know the "portion" that belongs to you and those that must serve purposes beyond you.

To help drive home this principle, let us quickly read a Bible passage. Pay attention to the emphasis on the word "portion" highlighted in the passage:

*"Behold that which I have seen: it is good and comely for one to eat and to drink, and to enjoy the good of all his labour that he taketh under the sun all the days of his life, which God giveth him: for it is his **portion**. Every man also to whom God hath given riches and wealth, and hath given him power to eat thereof, and to take his **portion**, and to rejoice in his labour; this is the gift of God"* (Ecc. 5:18–19).

Here is another Bible passage:

*"And the Lord said, Who then is that faithful and wise steward, whom his lord shall make ruler over his household, to give them their **portion** of meat in due season? Blessed is that servant, whom his lord when he cometh shall find so doing. Of a truth I say unto you, that he will make him ruler over all that he hath"* (Luke 12:42–44).

Here are other Bible passages on the concept of "portion": Gen. 31:14, Gen. 47:22, Lev. 6:17, 2 Chron. 31:16, Neh. 11:23, Isaiah 53:12, Ezek. 45:4–7, Ezek. 48:1–23.

As the Lord blesses you and entrusts you with greater riches than you need for your personal consumption, He will be doing so with other people, projects, and goals in mind. God, in His desire to touch lives, always looks for faithful people to work with and to work through. When He finds such people, He empowers them with wisdom, knowledge, anointing, vision, material riches, and other resources to carry out His mandates, to pursue His purpose, and to touch lives for the greater good of His Kingdom. You may be one of those people.

If God chooses to entrust you with riches in abundance, then learn to recognize which part of the wealth in your care is your "portion" and which parts He intends for you to spend outside of you. When it comes to enjoyment, you only have moral rights before God to use your *portion* in God and no more than your *portion*!

Using for your own pleasure that which God intends for others amounts to mismanagement, unfaithfulness, and bad stewardship. It is important for you to see the wealth entrusted in your hands as belonging to God, the Master, and true Owner. See

GOD'S WILL FOR YOUR EARTHLY RICHES

yourself as the caretaker simply executing the will of the true Owner. Your *portion* is His gift to you for your own enjoyment. You must use the rest to reach His goals!

God is generous enough to give you all that you need for maximum pleasure here on earth and for eternal pleasure after you leave this world. Therefore, learn and strive to be a faithful steward.

The Bible says:

"Moreover it is required in stewards, that a man be found faithful" (1 Cor. 4:2).

Do with God's money whatever He wants you to do with it. He is the Boss! He may give you excess money because He wants to take care of some orphans in your neighborhood or in a remote part of the earth, far from your present location. Obey Him. He may give you extra money because of a community or church project that He wishes to provide for. Listen to Him, and do as He says!

Some of the riches should serve to secure the financial future of your children. Do not deny them their inheritance. Others may belong to a missionary in need. Do not let such a missionary continue praying to God for provisions while you are holding back the portion belonging to him or her.

The children of Israel left Egypt with great riches. However, a great portion of their gold, silver, and other precious materials had to facilitate God's purpose for the Tabernacle. While in the wilderness, the Lord asked them to volunteer those materials for the work:

"And the LORD spake unto Moses, saying, Speak unto the children of Israel, that they bring me an offering: of every man that giveth it willingly with his heart ye shall take my offering. And this is the offering which ye shall take of them; gold, and silver, and brass, And blue, and purple, and scarlet, and fine linen, and goats' hair, And rams' skins dyed red, and badgers' skins, and shittim wood, Oil for the light, spices for anointing oil, and for sweet incense, Onyx stones, and stones to be set in the ephod, and in the breastplate. And let them make me a sanctuary; that I may dwell among them" (Ex. 25:1–8).

Recognize your portion, and do not delay God's purpose

Many people and purposes in the Kingdom suffer delays because those entrusted with the resources for them misuse the portions that God intended for such people and purposes.

Numerous projects in our churches do not take off because some people with the money intended for them choose to use God's budget differently. Once God's money gets into their hands, they simply forget that He is the true Owner and soon begin to act as lords over God's resources, ignoring His goals and serving their own selfish agendas. Such people do not represent the true spirit of faithfulness that is necessary for extending God's blessings to all of the families of the earth. They are unfaithful servants, hindering and delaying Gods plans.

How do you recognize which portion is yours and which must be distributed? How do you know how and when to distribute the other portions? These are important questions.

Your portion is that part that the Lord grants you the liberty to use for your own enjoyment and consumption within a specific

119

place, phase, and time of your life and in line with the standard of life that He approves for you. You will find true fulfillment and peace of mind while enjoying the portion that belongs to you, and you will feel deep inner conviction and correction when you attempt to use for your own desires the portions that belong to others.

Here are ways to recognize your portion in God:

- ✓ Your portion meets your needs in abundance but never wastefully.
- ✓ Your portion serves as a testimony of God's faithfulness.
- ✓ Your portion positions you to fulfill your destiny more effectively.
- ✓ Your portion rewards your efforts reasonably.
- ✓ Your portion glorifies God.

The subject of "portion" is very personal and distinct to each individual child of God. Therefore, we cannot compare two individual Christians based on lifestyle and standard of living. Do not try to copy other believers in this area. Learn to know your portion as an individual.

Your portion depends on your mission, mandate, and function. For example, a local evangelist operating in a rural community may need a comfortable and reliable bicycle for traveling while a hard-working evangelist in a city may need a comfortable and reliable car. They are both servants of God, but they do not have the same "portion" at the same time in terms of the level of income that each one of them needs. Their environments and "world" are different.

Another evangelist with a busy international schedule may

need to have the right budget to take care of his body by flying comfortably in the business class of commercial airlines. Individual needs are relative; hence, individual "portion" cannot be equal. Further, an evangelist traveling with a team of workers over long distances on a regular basis may need a private jet in order to serve God's purpose more effectively.

Without the proper understanding of this concept, we will criticize those that we think are living in luxury and will falsely accuse them of wasting resources while they are living within God's "portion" for their lives and enjoying the provisions necessary for their effectiveness. Learn to discern your portion, and avoid judging other people. When it comes to portion, God is the best judge of His children and His servants.

We are consciously using preachers to illustrate this concept of portion because of the unfair criticism and opposition that many of them face when God makes it possible for them to live comfortably.

The mandate and life's purpose determines the need, and the need determines the provisions and God's portion for a person. Our ministry titles do not necessarily determine our needs. Our mandates do. The pastor of a local church in a particular part of the world may need a larger "portion" than the bishop overseeing several churches in other parts of the world does.

Here is a Bible passage that puts it in perfect perspective:

"I have seen servants upon horses, and princes walking as servants upon the earth" (Ecc. 10:7).

Servants of rich people may seem to have "better" lives than royalty in certain places have. Ambassadors of some countries may live more comfortably than kings in some villages do. This is why it should not be a surprise to anyone to find God's children and *servants* living like royalty in this world. It is normal for God to make His children effective by providing for their needs.

Luxury is relative and subject to perception and environment

What we consider "luxury" is often relative and subject to perception and environment. One place may see a comfortable bicycle as luxurious. Another society may consider flying in business class as luxurious. Some circles may consider owning a private jet as luxury. Another circle may consider jet ownership a *necessity* and even a wise investment. God blesses His children with the intention of keeping them on top and keeping them effective in His purpose. He wants them to live for His glory and fulfill His mandates.

God normally takes care of His children by providing for their needs in a generous way (Phil. 4:19) so that they will stand out among their peers wherever they are and be the kind of people that others admire and sometimes envy.

Due to God's generosity, His supply of a person's "need" may appear excessive to many people. Servants of the Most High God may have portions from God that allow them to live better than ambassadors and political leaders in this world. God likes to have His children stand out. There is no reason why any believer should grumble over the goodness of God in the lives of other believers. We must learn to wish others well and be thankful to God for His goodness and faithfulness in their lives.

It is important to understand that what it takes to stand out in one part of the world or another community is not the same as what it might take to stand out in another environment. A person operating in a middle class neighborhood may need a higher monthly budget to stand out than someone else operating in a poor neighborhood does. The child of God with a mission to operate within an upper scale neighborhood will need a higher budget or "portion" in order to stand out in such a neighborhood. God is aware of such needs and provides for portions accordingly.

Those with larger vision and mandates need larger provisions. A person's "portion" in one phase of life may be different from the "portion" of the same person in another phase of life. A single man may need a different "portion" than a man that is married. The same married man will need a different "portion" when he begins to have children.

One person may need household staff, such as cooks, gardeners, cleaners, drivers, and so on, to avoid distractions and function effectively. Another person may not need such employees. Due to these differences, one person's lifestyle in the Kingdom may attract criticism from other people within or outside of the church that do not understand the place of portion in divine provisions.

We may not be qualified to judge the lifestyles of God's children unless the Lord Himself shows us that they are living outside of His will and instructs us to confront them about it. Even with such instructions, we have to speak to them personally, privately, respectfully, and lovingly. Such personal matters have no place in public discussions.

It is common these days to hear people condemn God's children and preachers for having their own private jets. However, a better understanding of the subject of portion will make such criticisms unnecessary in most cases.

There is nothing wrong with preachers or other believers having private jets if they make them more effective in what God wants them to do. In many cases, it can make financial sense and actually save money in addition to providing greater efficiency and comfort for some people to own their own airplanes.

Anyone traveling frequently with a large team on business or first class commercial flight tickets may need to consider the option of owning a private jet to save costs. If God considers it a person's "portion" to own a jet, the rest of God's people should celebrate God's goodness and be thankful to God for His faithfulness to such a person. Please let God's children enjoy their portions in God while you enjoy yours.

Let people enjoy their lives, and let God be the judge

Refrain from judging the servants of God in matters of direct personal accountability to God. God knows how to chastise them if they go outside of their bounds.

Unless preachers are cheating on their spouses, neglecting their children, leading people astray, defrauding people, or going against the word of God, it does the Kingdom more good for God's people to stay away from judging them. The world may persecute such servants of God because our world does not understand the way that God's Kingdom works, but God's children should know better.

Understand the importance of portion, and do not participate in judging people unnecessarily:

"Who art thou that judgest another man's servant? to his own master he standeth or falleth. Yea, he shall be holden up: for God is able to make him stand" (Rom. 14:4).

Bear in mind that God's portion in a person's life may also depend on the things that such a person left behind. God promised a hundred fold in return (Mark 10:28–30).

A person leaving a lucrative career to follow the Lord and receiving a hundred fold in return is likely to have a portion in life than is normal for the career that such a person left behind— and more! We should not consider it strange if one that would normally make a lot of money as a great motivational speaker in the world leaves the profession to follow the Lord and then makes at least double the income that similar speakers in the world make (1 Tim. 5:17).

The next time that you feel the temptation to judge people for their prosperity in God, take the time to think about their moneymaking potential in the world, and try to understand what they left behind.

A person's enjoyment can attract others to God

It should not matter to us if someone drives in an expensive car or lives in an expensive house.

The world is full of stories of people with humble beginnings experiencing God's blessings resulting in abundance. While others may criticize them for such lives of abundance and consider them wasteful, the fact is that they can actually attract and inspire other people with humble backgrounds. There are many preachers out there attracting people to the Lord because of their personal breakthroughs and victory over poverty.

Their abundance helps them to touch lives that they would not have touched if they had shown no visible signs of material success. Their visible success inspires and motivates others to get closer to God.

If one person's "luxurious" lifestyle inspires another person to fight against poverty, grow closer to God, and walk the path of earthly and eternal blessings, then we should wish to see more of God's children living in luxury! Many people judge others wrongly because of ignorance, and some judge purely out of jealousy and envy. They forget that God gives riches for strategic reasons.

If God blesses you and allows you to enjoy a large portion, do so openly and gladly. Remember that you owe no one any apologies for God's blessings in your life! Listen to your conscience, and avoid any lifestyle that you are uncomfortable with, whether it is with abundance or with lack. Learn to make sacrifices when you need to, and never consume any portion that does not belong to you.

Always put God first, and as much as you wish a great life for yourself, wish the same for others as well; be willing to help people in need as the Lord directs you.

"Jesus said unto him, Thou shalt love the Lord thy God with all thy heart, and with all thy soul, and with all thy mind. This is the first and great commandment. And the second is like unto it, Thou shalt love thy neighbor as thyself. On these two commandments hang all

the law and the prophets" (Matt. 22:37–40).

We wish people the very best in life when we walk in true love. The prosperity of others should give us reasons for celebration because it shows the goodness of God, and we know that God is able to use such prosperity to make eternal impact on the lives of other people.

Enjoy God's material blessings in your own life, and do not hesitate to let people know the secret of your success. Let them know that the Lord has been good to you, and invite them to come, taste, and see that the Lord is good! Your enjoyment of God's material blessings can put someone else on track with God.

Enjoy the portion that is yours, and consider it a privilege and an honor for God to entrust you with the portions that belong to others. Learn the joy of giving to others the portions that belong to them. Do not keep people waiting until tomorrow for the help that is within your power to render to them today (Prov. 3:28).

Holding back what you must give to others may frustrate God's purpose in their lives, and that will not please God. Learn to listen to the Lord's directions, and act on time. Give with gladness, and the Lord will entrust you with greater blessings.

Pursue true fulfillment

Fulfillment is the feeling we get when we accomplish the things that God wants us to do. True pleasure and life's greatest fulfillment belong to those that live and walk with God in a lifestyle that goes beyond meeting their personal needs. Enjoyment makes us happier people, but faithfulness makes us feel fulfilled. The pleasures of a hundred years of enjoyment are

127

little compared with one moment of true fulfillment!

God has far more than personal enjoyment in mind for you; He wants you to feel fulfilled in life! Pursue true fulfillment by discovering and following His plans for you. In the next chapter, we shall see one more reason why God wants you to have material riches.

7

GOD WANTS YOU TO BE RICH IN GOOD WORKS

"And he spake a parable unto them, saying, The ground of a certain rich man brought forth plentifully: And he thought within himself, saying, What shall I do, because I have no room where to bestow my fruits? And he said, This will I do: I will pull down my barns, and build greater; and there will I bestow all my fruits and my goods. And I will say to my soul, Soul, thou hast much goods laid up for many years; take thine ease, eat, drink, and be merry. But God said unto him, Thou fool, this night thy soul shall be required of thee: then whose shall those things be, which thou hast provided? So is he that layeth up treasure for himself, and is not rich toward God" (Luke 12:16–21).

In the last chapter, we saw the importance of enjoying God's blessings in our lives and concluded that we must look beyond our own personal enjoyments if we want to find true fulfillment in this life. We shall now proceed to see the importance of being rich in good works.

The Bible tells us that *"an innumerable multitude of people"* (Luke 12:1) were with the Lord Jesus when He gave the parable in our opening passage in this chapter. Most Bible students know that the Lord spoke general truths and principles when He taught the crowd and the deeper mysteries of the Kingdom when He spoke to His disciples in private.

Lessons presented before the crowd contain ideas and wisdom that must become part of our "common sense." In other words, they have to become the "normal" way for us to see things. It will be against common wisdom and rational behavior to live contrary to such instructions, as they are to be part of the acceptable minimum standard. Therefore, the subject of this chapter should become the normal part of our daily lives as we walk with God.

God wants you to be a blessing

While you must never apologize for enjoying the goodness of God in your life, you need to remember that God has other reasons beyond your personal enjoyment for wanting you to have earthly riches. As we saw in the previous chapter, it is important to identify the portion that He wants you to enjoy personally and those that you must use for other purposes. God blesses you so that you can enjoy His goodness and be a channel of His blessings. He wants to touch the families of the earth through you.

God made this point clear to Abraham thousands of years ago:

"And I will bless them that bless thee, and curse him that curseth thee: and in thee shall all families of the earth be blessed" (Gen. 12:3).

Most believers agree that they have access to God's blessings to Abraham through faith and sing the song, "Abraham's Blessings Are Mine." They are right in thinking so as we can see from the passages below:

"Know ye therefore that they which are of faith, the same are the children of Abraham. And the scripture, foreseeing that God would justify the heathen through faith, preached before the gospel unto Abraham, saying, In thee shall all nations be blessed. So then they which be of faith are blessed with faithful Abraham" (Gal. 3:7–9).

"For ye are all the children of God by faith in Christ Jesus. For as many of you as have been baptized into Christ have put on Christ. There is neither Jew nor Greek, there is neither bond nor free, there is neither male nor female: for ye are all one in Christ Jesus. And if ye be Christ's, then are ye Abraham's seed, and heirs according to the promise" (Gal. 3:26–29).

Unfortunately, many of those claiming God's promise to Abraham as theirs do not realize the responsibilities that follow the privileges of receiving God's blessings. The truth is that every believer embracing God's blessings through the promise to Abraham must also demonstrate commitment to God's *purpose* for Abraham. This purpose necessitated Abraham serving as instrument of God's blessing to the rest of the world. The true believer embracing God's promise of blessing to Abraham must also strive to be an instrument of blessing to the rest of the world.

God used Abraham to bring the Savior to the world, opening the door of salvation to humanity. The true Christian must identify with God's desire to see all people come to the knowledge of the truth by working and living to give every person on the planet access to the Gospel of salvation. The true believer is in this world to live in line with the will of God.

We must all develop passion to pursue God's mission for our lives by using material riches to make the world a better place while preparing people for eternity with God. Living to touch lives by doing the things that are good and right in the sight of God should be part of our normal lives.

What is your life's mission statement?

A mission statement is a summary of the purpose that you intend to fulfill, the mandate that you want to accomplish, or that cause for which you are willing to make all possible efforts to reach. While God wants you to enjoy His blessings in your life and He takes pleasure in watching you eat, drink, and be merry, He will not be pleased if you have no purpose in life beyond meeting your personal needs and wishes. He wants you to touch other lives and to prosper His Kingdom.

Every person should have a mission statement in life. Do you have one? If so, does your mission statement allow you to do more with your riches than just taking care of your personal need for enjoyment in this life? If not, then review your life's mission and (re)write your mission statement so that you can find true fulfillment in life. If you do not yet have a mission statement, write one as soon as possible.

The rich man in the parable of our opening passage had more harvest than his storage could hold. As he contemplated on what to do with the excess, he came up with a mission statement: *"eat, drink, and be merry."* He went on to tell himself, *"Soul, thou hast much goods laid up for many years."* He could not see any usefulness for his abundance beyond his personal need for enjoyment and relaxation.

God called this man a fool and decided to demand his soul from him that night. His mission statement was completely self-centered and practically useless to the greater purpose of God for allowing such abundance in his life. The unthankful man was determined to live a useless life, and his mentality displeased God.

There is more to life than eating, drinking, and rising up early to play (1 Cor. 10:7, Ex. 32:6). Anything outside of God's purpose that becomes a person's sole reason for living eventually becomes an idol! Those that pursue riches just for the sake of becoming rich without the higher purpose of making positive contributions to their world or pursuing dreams beyond their own personal needs eventually become slaves to riches and live unfulfilled lives.

We feel more fulfilled when we touch others

Pursuing money just for selfish reasons makes people end up with deep feelings of emptiness and loneliness on the inside, irrespective of how much wealth they gather, even if they have people around them, because they will lack the feeling of true fulfillment.

The Lord our Maker designed us to feel better with ourselves and with life when we are making positive contributions to our world, touching others for their own good, and helping people to experience His love through us. Meals are more enjoyable when eaten with others.

If you doubt it, then perform a simple experiment; go to the best restaurant that you can find in town, and order your favorite meal. Sit down there, and then eat alone. After a few days, call two or three people that you love and go out to eat together. Set a budget in place, and sponsor the meal. Observe the atmosphere at the table, the satisfaction on their faces, and their expression of gratitude at the end of the meal and then listen to your conscience. You will then know the difference between eating alone and sharing with others. Sharing will make you feel better.

While taking people out may sound more expensive, it will give you far more satisfaction. This is how your Maker created you! He made you to find true fulfillment when you cooperate with Him to touch other lives.

You can test this fact in many other ways:

Buy a precious new car, drive it alone, and then take someone with you for a ride, and you will see that it feels better to have someone else in that car with you. Pleasure feels better when shared with the people that we love.

Here is another experiment: Stand in front of a mirror, and tell the person there a great story. When you are done, stand before the right audience and tell the same story. Watch them pay attention, laugh, cry, think, and express the emotions and reactions applicable to such a story. Listen to them walk up to you at the end of the event to tell you what a difference your story made in their circumstances or how inspired they felt while listening to you, and you will understand the power and pleasure of sharing!

If you are a writer, a hundred unwritten books burning within you will never give you the satisfaction that you will get from a single book that you write and publish to share your inspiration with zealous readers around the world. There is fulfillment in sharing.

This is why people organize feasts and celebrate important milestones in their lives with others. We tend to enjoy more when we have others partake of our enjoyment (Luke 15:4–6, 8–9, 11–24).

Here is the question one more time: What is your life's mission statement? Make sure that it goes beyond "eat, drink, and be merry."

The Scripture declares, *"…It is written, That man shall not live by bread alone, but by every word of God"* (Luke 4:4). Follow God's instructions.

God's word says that He is blessing you so that He can bless the families of the earth through you. He wants you to be a blessing. It is therefore extremely important that you make your life's mission statement consistent with it. The most fulfilled man or woman on the planet is that person that is living in consistent sync with Heaven's purpose on earth and serving as the extension of God's hands and heart to a world in need.

Plan now to be rich in good works

When Paul the Apostle urged Timothy to instruct the believers about how to treat riches, he insisted on charging them to be rich in good works:

"Charge them that are rich in this world, that they be not highminded, nor trust in uncertain riches, but in the living God, who giveth us richly all things to enjoy; That they do good, that they be rich in good

works, ready to distribute, willing to communicate; Laying up in store for themselves a good foundation against the time to come, that they may lay hold on eternal life" (1 Tim. 6:17–19).

They must not become arrogant. They must trust in God and not in their riches. They must do well and be rich in good works, ready to share, and willing to touch lives. In this way, they would be laying a good foundation for themselves and preparing for eternal life.

The parable in our opening passage shows that the way a rich person treats riches can have eternal consequences for such a person. The man in the example lost his own soul!

Refusing to do the good that we know to do is considered sin (James 4:17, Luke 12:47–48), and it is wrong to ignore the plight of those that the Lord wants us to help. Therefore, make up your mind to be rich in good works.

How many people, places, projects, and causes do you want to facilitate in your lifetime? Take a moment to meditate and to pray for God's help as you plan and work towards leaving your mark on history by the grace of God.

Learn from the story of the rich man and Lazarus

"There was a certain rich man, which was clothed in purple and fine linen, and fared sumptuously every day: And there was a certain beggar named Lazarus, which was laid at his gate, full of sores, And desiring to be fed with the crumbs which fell from the rich man's table: moreover the dogs came and licked his sores. And it came to pass, that the beggar died, and was carried by the angels into Abraham's bosom: the rich man also died, and was buried; And in

hell he lift up his eyes, being in torments, and seeth Abraham afar off, and Lazarus in his bosom. And he cried and said, Father Abraham, have mercy on me, and send Lazarus, that he may dip the tip of his finger in water, and cool my tongue; for I am tormented in this flame. But Abraham said, Son, remember that thou in thy lifetime receivedst thy good things, and likewise Lazarus evil things: but now he is comforted, and thou art tormented. And beside all this, between us and you there is a great gulf fixed: so that they which would pass from hence to you cannot; neither can they pass to us, that would come from thence. Then he said, I pray thee therefore, father, that thou wouldest send him to my father's house: For I have five brethren; that he may testify unto them, lest they also come into this place of torment. Abraham saith unto him, They have Moses and the prophets; let them hear them. And he said, Nay, father Abraham: but if one went unto them from the dead, they will repent. And he said unto him, If they hear not Moses and the prophets, neither will they be persuaded, though one rose from the dead" (Luke 16:19–31).

The rich man in the story ended up spending eternity in pain, not because he was rich but because he was wicked! He had enough riches to enjoy exaggerated feasts daily, with enough crumbs falling from his table to feed a poor beggar at his gate, yet the dogs around him cared more about the condition of the beggar than he did. He was a rich wicked man!

He had sufficient money to have sent the poor man for medical treatment without feeling any pressure on his wealth, but he did not care! He was grossly wicked, and God could not help but alienate such a man from the ranks of the righteous and appoint him an eternal dwelling in the ultimate place of pain after his death. He did not take the time to think and realize that the poor beggar had any portion in the riches under his control. He wasted his riches while watching the man at his gate suffer in pain daily.

The rich man shut up his "bowels of compassion" (1 John 3:17) even when he had the opportunity to make a difference in the life of Lazarus. Consequently, he ended up in pain after his death and found himself denied a drop of water while he was in pain.

The Bible says:

"Whoso stoppeth his ears at the cry of the poor, he also shall cry himself, but shall not be heard" (Prov. 21:13).

While alive on earth, the rich man lived in material abundance and feasted daily, enjoying himself, but at death, he found himself begging for a drop of water! He wished he had known better and that he had lived better, but it was too late for him after death. He left his household with a bad example about how to handle material riches, and they were in danger of ending up in the same place of pain with him.

In his desire to prevent members of his household from ending up in the same pain, he requested Abraham to send Lazarus back to life on earth to warn his five brothers following his bad example, but Abraham could not grant such a request. It was too late!

His story should serve as a warning to anyone that is self-centered and wicked. Those living in pleasure should learn to pay attention to the needs of those living under pressure and wish their fellow human beings a life of pleasure as well. That is what God means by *"love thy neighbor as thyself"* (Matt. 22:39)! Wish for others what you wish for yourself. The rich man had material riches, but he was poor in good works.

We must always live in this world with eternity in mind and remember the words of the preacher in the book of Ecclesiastes:

"Let us hear the conclusion of the whole matter: Fear God, and keep his commandments: for this is the whole duty of man. For God shall bring every work into judgment, with every secret thing, whether it be good, or whether it be evil" (Ecc. 12:13–14).

Live your life on earth to have a clear conscience toward God and towards man so that you will never have any reasons to fear when you will have to stand before the judgment seat of Christ!

In the story, Lazarus, the beggar, had a tough life on earth, but he ended up in pleasure after his death. His days of pain were over, and his new life would remain for eternity!

Some scholars wrongly use this story to encourage poverty, claiming that the rich man ended up in the place of pain because of his riches and that the poor man ended up in the place of pleasure because of his poverty. Their position wrongly assumes that material riches in this world lead to eternal pain while poverty in this world leads to eternal pleasure.

There is nothing in the passage to suggest that Lazarus ended up in Abraham's bosom because of his poverty or that the rich man ended up in pain because of his riches. The rich man was wicked, and Lazarus, under extreme pressure from lack of material supplies, would rather beg than steal. Therefore, their eternity neither depended on riches nor on poverty but on their conduct while alive. It is also possible to be rich and righteous and to be poor and wicked!

Job was rich, righteous, and rich in good works

The story of Job in the Bible shows us a man who went through immense trials. Job was not sure of the reasons for the ordeal and the terrible experiences that he went through within a relatively short time. He was a rich man who lost virtually everything during a tough time of sudden trial.

In his effort to identify possible causes for his ordeal, he examined different areas of his life to see what he might have done against God to deserve the evil that he was experiencing. Personal attitude towards riches was one of the areas that he examined. He wanted to be sure that he had touched other lives positively and in line with God's expectations.

Everyone entrusted with riches today can learn God's expectations for their riches by paying close attention to Job's self-examination here:

"If I did despise the cause of my manservant or of my maidservant, when they contended with me; What then shall I do when God riseth up? and when he visiteth, what shall I answer him? Did not he that made me in the womb make him? and did not one fashion us in the womb? If I have withheld the poor from their desire, or have caused the eyes of the widow to fail; Or have eaten my morsel myself alone, and the fatherless hath not eaten thereof; (For from my youth he was brought up with me, as with a father, and I have guided her from my mother's womb;) If I have seen any perish for want of clothing, or any poor without covering; If his loins have not blessed me, and if he were not warmed with the fleece of my sheep; If I have lifted up my hand against the fatherless, when I saw my help in the gate: Then let mine arm fall from my shoulder blade, and mine arm be broken from the

bone" (Job 31:13–22).

The self-examination above shows that Job paid personal attention to the needs of poor people. He took care of widows and orphans. He also understood the importance of being considerate in his dealings with his servants. He did not use his position of power to cheat them. One of the ways to identify people of integrity is to pay attention to how they treat their subordinates and others that are in vulnerable positions under their care. Wicked people take advantage of the weak, and righteous people treat other human beings with a sense of dignity and respect.

Job was rich in good works, and he knew that doing otherwise could invoke God's anger in his life. As God prospers you and gives you more than you will ever need, strive to be rich in good works.

Doing good to others when you find the opportunity should be part of your normal life. As we have seen earlier, the Lord Jesus spoke in the opening passage to the crowd, meaning that He was teaching them basic or general truth that should be part of "common sense" for every normal and rational person.

Tabitha was rich in good works

One of the most heart-touching stories in the book of Acts is that of a disciple named Tabitha. She exemplified good works. Tabitha was an active member of the church in Joppa before dying of an illness. Her death touched the entire congregation and turned out to be one of the most sorrowful and emotional moments in the lives of the widows in the church there because she dedicated her life to caring for these women, making coats and garments for them.

As a result, the widows could not afford to see her leave this world. She meant too much in their lives, and they needed her around.

Moved by the reaction of these widows, the church sent messengers to Peter in Lydda, asking him to join them in Joppa immediately. They needed God to intervene in the situation.

Here is a portion of the story:

"Now there was at Joppa a certain disciple named Tabitha, which by interpretation is called Dorcas: this woman was full of good works and almsdeeds which she did. And it came to pass in those days, that she was sick, and died: whom when they had washed, they laid her in an upper chamber. And forasmuch as Lydda was nigh to Joppa, and the disciples had heard that Peter was there, they sent unto him two men, desiring him that he would not delay to come to them. Then Peter arose and went with them. When he was come, they brought him into the upper chamber: and all the widows stood by him weeping, and shewing the coats and garments which Dorcas made, while she was with them" (Acts 9:36–39).

Notice the Bible's description of this woman: *"full of good works and almsdeeds."* She was rich in good works. The widows surrounded her dead body, crying and desiring her to live. Her death brought them real pain because her life had brought them true gain!

Peter prayed, and God released her back to the widows, alive!

"But Peter put them all forth, and kneeled down, and prayed; and

turning him to the body said, Tabitha, arise. And she opened her eyes: and when she saw Peter, she sat up. And he gave her his hand, and lifted her up, and when he had called the saints and widows, presented her alive. And it was known throughout all Joppa; and many believed in the Lord" (Acts 9:40–42).

Her story is a classic example of what the Bible says about the reaction of people towards the death of a righteous person. It is in great contrast with how people respond to the death of the wicked:

"When it goeth well with the righteous, the city rejoiceth: and when the wicked perish, there is shouting" (Prov. 11:10).

Make up your mind to touch lives with your life. Show your world the true love of God, and always make sure that people in need have reasons to celebrate coming in contact with you. God wants you to use earthly riches to touch lives in this world and to be rich in good works.

Cornelius got Heaven's attention

"There was a certain man in Caesarea called Cornelius, a centurion of the band called the Italian band, A devout man, and one that feared God with all his house, which gave much alms to the people, and prayed to God alway. He saw in a vision evidently about the ninth hour of the day an angel of God coming in to him, and saying unto him, Cornelius. And when he looked on him, he was afraid, and said, What is it, Lord? And he said unto him, Thy prayers and thine alms are come up for a memorial before God. And now send men to Joppa, and call for one Simon, whose surname is Peter: He

lodgeth with one Simon a tanner, whose house is by the sea side: he shall tell thee what thou oughtest to do" (Acts 10:1–6).

This man was not only a devout man of prayer. He *"gave much alms to the people"* and got Heaven's attention! *"Thy prayers and thine alms are come up for a memorial before God"* he heard an angel announce. That must have been very encouraging for him to hear.

The Bible says that God does not forget the things that we do for love, in His name:

"For God is not unrighteous to forget your work and labour of love, which ye have shewed toward his name, in that ye have ministered to the saints, and do minister" (Heb. 6:10).

The combination of his devout lifestyle, prayer, and alms made him the kind of person that God was comfortable to work with.

He qualified himself as a channel of God's blessings, making his household the first to receive the baptism of the Holy Spirit and opening the door for other Gentiles to have similar spiritual experience with God. Those that are not faithful with material blessings often deny themselves opportunities for greater spiritual blessings (Luke 16:11).

"While Peter yet spake these words, the Holy Ghost fell on all them which heard the word. And they of the circumcision which believed were astonished, as many as came with Peter, because that on the Gentiles also was poured out the gift of the Holy Ghost. For they heard them speak with tongues, and magnify God. Then answered Peter, Can any man forbid water, that these should not be baptized, which have received the Holy Ghost as well as we? And he

commanded them to be baptized in the name of the Lord. Then prayed they him to tarry certain days" (Acts 10:44–48).

This man lived in a time when the believers expected only the Jews to experience the baptism of the Holy Spirit, but his lifestyle got God's attention and changed that perception!

Saved by grace to do good works

Many believers, realizing that the Lord saved us by grace and not by our good works, are undermining the importance of doing good works. This is wrong! The Bible shows that God saved us by grace and left us in this world to do good works:

"For we are his workmanship, created in Christ Jesus unto good works, which God hath before ordained that we should walk in them" (Eph. 2:10).

The Lord Jesus made it clear that we have to shine the light in this world and attract people to our Heavenly Father by doing good works:

"Let your light so shine before men, that they may see your good works, and glorify your Father which is in heaven" (Matt. 5:16).

Our world needs to see that we are doing good works. They need to see us take care of widows, orphans, strangers, and others in need. We need to speak for those that cannot speak for themselves and defend the rights of those that cannot defend themselves. We must let God's riches in our lives serve God's intentions for the people that He cares for.

Good works mean different things to different people

depending on their personal needs. To a person in prison, "good works" can mean going to visit such a person and/or making it possible for others to visit them. To those that are naked, "good works" can mean supplying clothes to them. To those that are hungry, "good works" means providing the food that they need.

It is extremely important to God that we meet people at the point of their needs. Read Matthew 25:31–45 to get it in the Lord's own words, and you will see that God takes this subject personally!

In many situations, people recognize God's love better through actions than in words:

"But whoso hath this world's good, and seeth his brother have need, and shutteth up his bowels of compassion from him, how dwelleth the love of God in him? My little children, let us not love in word, neither in tongue; but in deed and in truth" (1 John 3:17–18).

"If a brother or sister be naked, and destitute of daily food, And one of you say unto them, Depart in peace, be ye warmed and filled; notwithstanding ye give them not those things which are needful to the body; what doth it profit? Even so faith, if it hath not works, is dead, being alone" (James 2:15–17).

The Bible consistently encourages us to do good works:

"But to do good and to communicate forget not: for with such sacrifices God is well pleased" (Heb. 13:16).

"And let us not be weary in well doing: for in due season we shall reap, if we faint not. As we have therefore opportunity, let us do good unto all men, especially unto them who are of the household of faith"

(Gal. 6:9–10).

"This is a faithful saying, and these things I will that thou affirm constantly, that they which have believed in God might be careful to maintain good works. These things are good and profitable unto men" (Titus 3:8).

The Lord Jesus paid the ultimate price to reconcile us back to God and left us here to do good works:

"Who gave himself for us, that he might redeem us from all iniquity, and purify unto himself a peculiar people, zealous of good works. These things speak, and exhort, and rebuke with all authority. Let no man despise thee" (Titus 2:14–15).

Notice the phrase "zealous unto good works." This means that God wants us to do good works with eagerness, enthusiasm, fervor, and strong determination. In other words, doing good works should be part of the things that we enjoy to do in this life. Therefore, touch lives gladly!

8

GOD WANTS YOU TO LEAVE AN INHERITANCE FOR GENERATIONS!

"A good man leaveth an inheritance to his children's children: and the wealth of the sinner is laid up for the just" (Prov. 13:22)

Here is something else that God wants you to do with your material riches - leave an inheritance for your children's children or for generations beyond your time.

Another word for inheritance is legacy. Inheritance has to do with ownership or succession by heredity. It is something that one gains ownership of because of one's relationship or connection with a person or a body of persons. An inheritance can be in the form of real estate property, such as land and houses, or intellectual property, such as rights to concepts, inventions, songs, books, and so on. An inheritance can also be a reputation or a great name. An inheritance can be a vision or life's mission as well.

Many people struggle under financial pressure unnecessarily for too long because they began their journey towards material success with little or practically nothing. Their parents left nothing of significant material value for them to give them a head start in life. Such people spend several years walking around with great business ideas while lacking the financial resources needed to execute such ideas. They struggle to make ends meet and work hard to get the most basic things of life because no one left any lucrative legacy or inheritance for them.

Others, blessed with an inheritance, go through life on the faster lane. The money to finance their college education was available before they were born. Their families had huge possessions of land, houses, and businesses waiting for them to take over and carry on to the next generation. They had access to the best education available and received training to lead their world. Their family names open new doors, and the reputation of their parents serve as collateral in new ventures. Theirs is a life set up for accelerated progress!

While everyone must pay some kind of price for their own success, those blessed with a reasonable inheritance often have the advantage of a head start in life. God is aware of this fact, and He wants His children to be conscious of it as well. That is why He wants the righteous to leave an inheritance for generations ahead. This is part of His strategy for prospering the descendants of faithful believers.

Understanding God's purpose for inheritance will help you to pave the way for generations to come, whether you have children of your own or not. Those that have no children should adopt one or more or adopt a vision, a cause, a community, a church, a people, a dream, or an organization and apply the principles in this chapter to such "children."

Learn to see God's perspective

When you walk with God, He does not only want you to succeed in life, He actually wants your children to succeed as well. Your hard work should make life easier for them. Your experience, wisdom, wealth, purity, fame, education, exposure, and all of the other great things that God has blessed you with should be carried on to those that will follow you.

Your descendants are then to improve on everything that they receive from you and leave a greater inheritance to the next generation so that the Lord's goodness will continue from one generation to the next.

Build and use material riches with at least three generations in mind: your generation, your children's generation, and their children's generation.

When this happens, you will be fulfilling the following scriptures about the just person:

"The just man walketh in his integrity: his children are blessed after him" (Prov. 20:7).

"His seed shall be mighty upon earth: the generation of the upright shall be blessed" (Psa 112:2).

"His soul shall dwell at ease; and his seed shall inherit the earth" (Ps.

25:13).

God's promises in your life are also for your children in the same way that God blessed the children of Abraham:

"And I will make thee exceeding fruitful, and I will make nations of thee, and kings shall come out of thee. And I will establish my covenant between me and thee and thy seed after thee in their generations for an everlasting covenant, to be a God unto thee, and to thy seed after thee. And I will give unto thee, and to thy seed after thee, the land wherein thou art a stranger, all the land of Canaan, for an everlasting possession; and I will be their God" (Gen. 17:6–8).

"For the promise is unto you, and to your children, and to all that are afar off, even as many as the LORD our God shall call" (Acts 2:39).

God knew that the future of His plan to bless the families of the earth depended not only on His blessings on the life of Abraham but also on Abraham's ability to pass such blessings down to his children.

God had confidence in Abraham's commitment towards His purpose. He knew that the man would train his children to walk in the ways of God:

"And the LORD said, Shall I hide from Abraham that thing which I do; Seeing that Abraham shall surely become a great and mighty nation, and all the nations of the earth shall be blessed in him? For I know him, that he will command his children and his household after him, and they shall keep the way of the LORD, to do justice and judgment; that the LORD may bring upon Abraham that which he hath spoken of him" (Gen. 18:17–19)

The work of God on the earth is like running in a relay race. One runner takes the baton to the next runner, and the work progresses according to the speed and effectiveness of those running in the race. One person's failure has the potential to slow things down for those ahead and has the potential to affect the success and reputation of the entire team. On the other hand, the success of one person can make it a lot easier for the entire team to win.

You and your children are part of God's relay team, and you need to ensure that those receiving the baton from you get special advantages in the race so that they can move ahead and give the baton to the next generation.

Follow the good example of Abraham:

"And Abraham gave all that he had unto Isaac" (Gen. 25:5).

Learn to think in terms of generations

Let us revisit the opening passage and break it down for a moment:

"A good man leaveth an inheritance to his children's children: and the wealth of the sinner is laid up for the just" (Prov. 13:22).

Learn to think in terms of generations, and plan well. Some people only live for the moment and make shortsighted decisions, but everyone with the proper understanding of God's plans must think further. We have to weigh the effects of our actions and inactions, not just in the light of today but also in view of tomorrow, weeks to come, months to come, years to come, several generations, and eternity!

We need to think about making a positive impact on those that will follow our footsteps, carry the same last names, hold the same passports, serve in the same professions, and much more. We can make things easier or more difficult for them depending on how we plan and live our lives.

As mentioned earlier, leaving an inheritance for your children's children implies that your riches must benefit at least three generations. It has to, at the very least, benefit you, your children, and the children of your children - a total of three generations!

Having your children start life from an advantaged position increases the likelihood that they will succeed faster and influence their generation for God. Parenting is not complete without giving children the keys and the resources that they need to be able to stand firm, to be significant in their world, and to fulfill God's purposes for their lives.

Many Christians that are passionate about the subject of material prosperity often quote the second part of the passage above, *"the wealth of the sinner is laid up for the just,"* and take it to simply mean that God's people will be possessing the wealth that the people outside of the church now control.

Some have suggested that by praying harder and sowing seeds into some ministries, they will automatically take possession of the wealth of the rest of the world, but it is not as easy as that. With God, lasting progress requires strategic planning and diligent commitment over time. That is why we must all learn to think ahead.

While it is clear that God has the ability to bless one with riches suddenly, an attentive student of the Bible reading the verse above would see a connection between the first part of the verse and the second part.

When good people leave an inheritance for their children and give them the necessary advantage of beginning well, their children will be in the position to take control of the wealth that is laid up for them in their world, beating their peers and outperforming others in their generations. The first part of the verse, namely, "*A good man leaveth an inheritance to his children's children,*" is an important key to the fulfillment of the second.

It takes generational thinking to achieve most of God's greater plans for His people and for His Kingdom. That is why God often speaks in terms of generations:

"And they shall build the old wastes, they shall raise up the former desolations, and they shall repair the waste cities, the desolations of many generations. And strangers shall stand and feed your flocks, and the sons of the alien shall be your plowmen and your vinedressers. But ye shall be named the Priests of the LORD: men shall call you the Ministers of our God: ye shall eat the riches of the Gentiles, and in their glory shall ye boast yourselves" (Is. 61:4–6).

In addition to enjoying the fruits of your labor and taking care of the needs of those around you, make conscious efforts to think beyond your time and to lay the foundation for generations to come. Good people think beyond themselves. Make up your mind to provide more advantages in life for your children than you have been able to enjoy. By doing so, you will be prospering the Kingdom of God beyond your time.

Knowing that you need to leave a legacy for at least two more generations will help you to raise the standard and to redefine how rich you *need* to be. If we only live to pay our monthly bills and survive from paycheck to paycheck, then we are living below God's plans for our material riches and need to target a higher income.

We must set financial goals that include enjoying life, touching lives, leaving an inheritance for generations to come, and being instrumental to the advancement of the Kingdom of God in our time. We must refuse and renounce any and every teaching that makes us settle for less!

Define your legacies

How do you want history to remember you?

David served his generation in the will of God before he died:

"For David, after he had served his own generation by the will of God, fell on sleep, and was laid unto his fathers, and saw corruption" (Acts 13:36).

He also prepared the way for his son, Solomon, to build the temple by making the vision clear, defeating the enemies of the land, establishing strategic relationships, and by making material resources available for the work. His efforts made the burden of the work lighter for Solomon.

Here is how the Bible puts it:

"Then David gave to Solomon his son the pattern of the porch, and of the houses thereof, and of the treasuries thereof, and of the upper chambers thereof, and of the inner parlours thereof, and of the place

of the mercy seat, And the pattern of all that he had by the spirit, of the courts of the house of the LORD, and of all the chambers round about, of the treasuries of the house of God, and of the treasuries of the dedicated things: Also for the courses of the priests and the Levites, and for all the work of the service of the house of the LORD, and for all the vessels of service in the house of the LORD. He gave of gold by weight for things of gold, for all instruments of all manner of service; silver also for all instruments of silver by weight, for all instruments of every kind of service: Even the weight for the candlesticks of gold, and for their lamps of gold, by weight for every candlestick, and for the lamps thereof: and for the candlesticks of silver by weight, both for the candlestick, and also for the lamps thereof, according to the use of every candlestick. And by weight he gave gold for the tables of shewbread, for every table; and likewise silver for the tables of silver: Also pure gold for the fleshhooks, and the bowls, and the cups: and for the golden basons he gave gold by weight for every bason; and likewise silver by weight for every bason of silver: And for the altar of incense refined gold by weight; and gold for the pattern of the chariot of the cherubims, that spread out their wings, and covered the ark of the covenant of the LORD" (1 Chron. 28:11–18).

Apart from the preparations that he made for the temple, David also left Solomon with real estate properties, a great name, and a special covenant with God. In addition, he gave his children outstanding instructions to help them walk in the fear of the Lord. David's legacy went beyond three generations. We are still enjoying his efforts several generations later by singing the songs that he wrote. Many Gospel singers are still making money by singing songs from his psalms today! His success transcended several generations. God wants you to bless generations!

Some names open doors, and other names close doors. Leave a good name for those coming after you. Always remember, wherever you are and whatever you do, that you are paving the way for others. You represent your faith, your family, your nation, your profession, your association, your district, your church, your race, your gender, and so on, whether you are conscious of it or not. You are an ambassador, and your life always leaves a mark and a legacy, good or bad, whether you like it or not!

We cannot overemphasize the importance of leaving a good name for your children. As you consider leaving riches for your offspring, make up your mind to help them find favor with God and with men by leaving them a good name:

"A good name is rather to be chosen than great riches, and loving favour rather than silver and gold" (Prov. 22:1)

Prepare your heirs

An heir is an inheritor, a beneficiary of an inheritance, a successor, or the recipient of an inheritance. Most people pass their inheritance to their children through a legal document containing their wishes called a *testament* or *will*. A testament usually takes effect after the death of the testator.

"For where a testament is, there must also of necessity be the death of the testator. For a testament is of force after men are dead: otherwise it is of no strength at all while the testator liveth" (Heb. 9:16–17).

Due to the general understanding that testaments take effect after a person's death, people have the natural tendency to associate inheritance only with the future. They think that they simply need to make sure that they have material wealth stored up for their children and everything will be just fine. That is not the case.

The fact is that it takes more than material riches to secure the future for a new generation. Heirs must have the vision, the training, and the grace to carry on God's mission for the wealth that they inherit. Therefore, their preparation must start from the day of their birth. They must receive the training necessary to shoulder great responsibilities, manage great wealth, and do greater things with and for God. They need the right training to fear God and to be smart, hardworking, disciplined, committed, consistent, wise, and industrious.

The Bible says:

"Train up a child in the way he should go: and when he is old, he will not depart from it" (Prov. 22:6).

The process of conveying inheritance from one generation to the next must include the preparation of qualified successors. They must learn to, at least, think as responsible and successful people with a mandate to bless the families of the earth and to glorify God with their lives and the material riches passed on to them. *Effective parenting* is therefore an important part of the entire process.

Training is essential for success, and no one is qualified to handle an inheritance without the right training. Remember that the heir must carry on the inheritance to the next generation. Simply being a son or daughter is not enough to help a person carry on a legacy from one generation to the next. Success is not just in the blood. A servant with the right character has the potential to rule over an untrained son and to control a testator's estate.

"A wise servant shall have rule over a son that causeth shame, and shall have part of the inheritance among the brethren" (Prov. 17:2).

Heirs must be wiser than servants are if they are to succeed! Therefore, train your successors properly. Qualify them to rule effectively. Prepare them to expand your legacy and convey your inheritance to generations beyond their time.

It is important for them to have the spiritual, moral, and intellectual capacities necessary to manage, grow, and multiply the wealth that you leave for them. This prepares the way for them to lead their world and, to in turn, leave an inheritance for generations after them. Give them the best and most appropriate education to help them develop their unique gifts and talents and to ensure that they have the expertise essential for fulfilling the plan of God for their lives.

Train them in character, and make sure that they understand important principles of life and progress, such as faithfulness, accountability, responsibility, the fear of the Lord, self-control, honor, respect, legacy, commitment, sowing and reaping, hard work, planning, discipline, budgeting, sacrifice, service, integrity, negotiations, marketing, and much more.

Leaving huge material riches in the hands of a person that has no character to value and utilize it properly can lead to the destruction of both the person and the wealth. Therefore, invest in training the character of future generations to ensure that the heirs are ready for their time:

"Now I say, That the heir, as long as he is a child, differeth nothing from a servant, though he be lord of all; But is under tutors and governors until the time appointed of the father" (Gal. 4:1–2).

Let them understand God's purpose for wealth and follow His principles for material wealth utilization, preservation, and multiplication. Just like you, or even better, they must also understand the importance of empowering generations after them.

The proverbial prodigal son in the Bible received his inheritance before he was mature enough to handle it, and it did him no good! He traveled to a far country, wasted it on prostitutes, and found himself destitute. You can read the story in Luke 15:11–32. Prepare your successors well ahead of the time when they will be in charge of the material blessings.

The value of family inheritance

Many people underestimate the importance of preserving their family inheritance, but God's people must be different. We live in a time when people want instant gratification and do not mind spending tomorrow's money today, building up debts for the next generation to pay. God's children have to set better examples. They must be willing to do whatever it takes to pass blessings on from one generation to the next.

In the Bible, Naboth understood this principle and risked his life to preserve the inheritance of his family for the next generation. To the readers that may not be familiar with the Bible story, Naboth lived in Israel in the days of King Ahab, and his family had a fruitful vineyard near the King's palace. The vineyard was attractive, and the location was favorable.

For personal convenience, Ahab offered to buy Naboth's vineyard or exchange it with him for another vineyard. The king promised giving him a better one or paying money to have it.

Here is the passage:

"And it came to pass after these things, that Naboth the Jezreelite had a vineyard, which was in Jezreel, hard by the palace of Ahab king of Samaria. And Ahab spake unto Naboth, saying, Give me thy vineyard, that I may have it for a garden of herbs, because it is near unto my house: and I will give thee for it a better vineyard than it; or, if it seem good to thee, I will give thee the worth of it in money" (1 Kings 21:1–2).

However, Naboth, determined to preserve the vineyard as part of his family inheritance, turned down the king's offer.

"And Naboth said to Ahab, The LORD forbid it me, that I should give the inheritance of my fathers unto thee" (1 Kings 21:3)

Where did Naboth find the courage to say "no" to the king of the land? Why was he able to resist the temptation of a "better vineyard" or money? The answer is simple. He understood the plan of God and knew that God wanted him to preserve the family's inheritance.

Naboth was mindful of God's instructions in the Holy Scriptures:

"Neither shall the inheritance remove from one tribe to another tribe; but every one of the tribes of the children of Israel shall keep himself to his own inheritance" (Num. 36:9).

"Moreover the prince shall not take of the people's inheritance by oppression, to thrust them out of their possession; but he shall give his

sons inheritance out of his own possession: that my people be not scattered every man from his possession" (Ezek. 46:18).

The situation between Ahab and Naboth did not end with Naboth's refusal. Refusing a king's demand was not a light matter in those days, and one can imagine that Naboth was aware of the risks and the possible consequences. Naboth's refusal was the beginning of a big and prolonged trouble in the kingdom, and Israel was never the same from that moment on!

After Naboth's refusal, the king went back home feeling sad and humiliated. He even went on a hunger strike. That must have been a special land! His evil wife, Jezebel, uncomfortable with her husband's sorrow, consoled him and promised to get the land for the king.

Here is the Bible's account:

"But Jezebel his wife came to him, and said unto him, Why is thy spirit so sad, that thou eatest no bread? And he said unto her, Because I spake unto Naboth the Jezreelite, and said unto him, Give me thy vineyard for money; or else, if it please thee, I will give thee another vineyard for it: and he answered, I will not give thee my vineyard. And Jezebel his wife said unto him, Dost thou now govern the kingdom of Israel? arise, and eat bread, and let thine heart be merry: I will give thee the vineyard of Naboth the Jezreelite" (1 Kings 21:5–7).

Jezebel worked up a successful plan to kill Naboth and then asked her husband to go and take the vineyard after the innocent man's death. Ahab followed his wife's instructions and went there hoping to possess it, but God could not tolerate such an evil act!

God was angry, and He pronounced judgment on the house of

Ahab.

This was not the first thing that the king had done against God. King Ahab did many things to provoke God's anger before this time, yet lived. We know that he married a princess from Zidon who worshipped idols, introduced Baal worship in the land, flooded the country with Baal priests, allowed the killing of many of the prophets of God, and corrupted the hearts of God's people, yet God allowed him to live.

However, killing a man that stood with God on the subject of family inheritance was just another evil too much! God had enough of Ahab, and it was time for divine judgment.

The king did not only disregard the condition of God's people under his leadership. Ahab also showed by this single act that he was willing to disregard the future of God's people by breaking the law of inheritance as well. God made a final judgment; Ahab had to die!

"And it came to pass, when Ahab heard that Naboth was dead, that Ahab rose up to go down to the vineyard of Naboth the Jezreelite, to take possession of it. And the word of the LORD came to Elijah the Tishbite, saying, Arise, go down to meet Ahab king of Israel, which is in Samaria: behold, he is in the vineyard of Naboth, whither he is gone down to possess it. And thou shalt speak unto him, saying, Thus saith the LORD, Hast thou killed, and also taken possession? And thou shalt speak unto him, saying, Thus saith the LORD, In the place where dogs licked the blood of Naboth shall dogs lick thy blood, even thine. And Ahab said to Elijah, Hast thou found me, O mine enemy? And he answered, I have found thee: because thou hast sold thyself to work evil in the sight of the LORD. Behold, I will bring evil upon thee, and will take away thy posterity, and will cut off from

Ahab him that pisseth against the wall, and him that is shut up and left in Israel, And will make thine house like the house of Jeroboam the son of Nebat, and like the house of Baasha the son of Ahijah, for the provocation wherewith thou hast provoked me to anger, and made Israel to sin. And of Jezebel also spake the LORD, saying, The dogs shall eat Jezebel by the wall of Jezreel. Him that dieth of Ahab in the city the dogs shall eat; and him that dieth in the field shall the fowls of the air eat" (1 Kings 21:16–24).

God takes this subject seriously, and so must we!

Do not despise birthrights

Being born into a godly family should have certain privileges, rights, and responsibilities. Birthrights should have special advantages. The children of righteous parents should have spiritual and material advantages over other children. God wants His children to have the inheritance that belongs to them. That is why He will gladly give you more riches than you will ever need in your lifetime. He wants your children to benefit from their connection to you.

In the Bible, Esau was born with a birthright superior to that of his brother, Jacob, but he despised it and sold it to his brother for a plate of food! Esau was entitled to the double portion of his father's inheritance because he was the first-born son of the family. Jacob did not have that kind of right, but he had great appreciation for the birthright.

"And Esau said to Jacob, Feed me, I pray thee, with that same red pottage; for I am faint: therefore was his name called Edom. And Jacob said; Sell me this day thy birthright. And Esau said, Behold, I am at the point to die: and what profit shall this birthright do to

me?" (Gen. 25:30–32).

Seeing how Esau was to despise his birthright, God preferred Jacob:

"As it is written, Jacob have I loved, but Esau have I hated" (Rom. 9:13).

God wants you to leave sustainable inheritance for generations after you. Prepare your legacy, and begin to make sure that your successors are ready for the great things that you and the Lord have ahead of them. Teach them to value and appreciate their birthrights. This is part of God's plan and will for your material riches.

9

GOD WANTS YOU TO PROSPER HIS KINGDOM

"And it came to pass, when the king sat in his house, and the LORD had given him rest round about from all his enemies; That the king said unto Nathan the prophet, See now, I dwell in an house of cedar, but the ark of God dwelleth within curtains. And Nathan said to the king, Go, do all that is in thine heart; for the LORD is with thee" (2 Sam. 7:1–3).

We have seen that God wants you to have material riches so that you can serve as His representative, enjoy life, touch lives by doing good works, and leave an inheritance for generations to come. We shall now look at one more reason why God wants you to have earthly riches: namely, so that you can prosper His Kingdom in this world.

Prospering God's Kingdom will require one to have a heart after God, have the resources to prosper the Kingdom, and the understanding to see things from God's perspective.

The opening passage in this chapter is a portion from the life of one of the greatest kings of all time. King David had a great heart for God, and he prospered God's work beyond his lifetime. Let us begin this chapter by learning a few things from David's heart and mentality.

Inspirations from David's heart for God

David killed a lion and a bear in a time when such deeds could have propelled him into regional fame and stardom, yet he was unknown in the community and was of little significance in his own family. This is because he did not try to be in the limelight. He was simply carrying out his tasks, tending to his family's flock faithfully. He killed the lion and the bear to protect the family's animals. His strong sense of responsibility pushed him to risk his own life more than once. He did not really seek for fame.

Although David was not in the spotlight, God knew him because our God sees everything, including those things that take place behind the scenes. God loved David's sense of responsibility and dedication to duty. David also had a special heart for God, and God decided to make him king in the land in place of King Saul. Saul had become too self-centered and careless about the will of God, forcing the Lord to reject Saul and choose David.

"And Samuel said to Saul, Thou hast done foolishly: thou hast not kept the commandment of the LORD thy God, which he commanded thee: for now would the LORD have established thy kingdom upon Israel for ever. But now thy kingdom shall not continue: the LORD hath sought him a man after his own heart, and the LORD hath commanded him to be captain over his people, because thou hast not kept that which the LORD commanded thee" (1 Sam. 13:13–14).

Saul was a shy and simple man before God chose him to serve as king in the land, but he soon became obsessed with the desire for approval from the crowd, making it easier for him to please the people than to please God. He ended up in disobedience to God. Consequently, the Lord rejected him as king and chose David to serve in his place. Samuel the prophet prayed for God to retain Saul as king, but the Lord's decision was final. It was too late for Saul.

"And the LORD said unto Samuel, How long wilt thou mourn for Saul, seeing I have rejected him from reigning over Israel? fill thine horn with oil, and go, I will send thee to Jesse the Bethlehemite: for I have provided me a king among his sons" (1 Sam. 16:1).

David had the kind of heart that God was looking for, and the Lord decided to make him king.

As a king, David was successful by every human yardstick. His enemies had either been defeated or had concluded that fighting against him would be suicidal. The king had peace, fame, admiration, honor, and riches. Most men in his position would have simply decided to sit back, relax, and enjoy the rest of their lives, thanking God for His kindness all through the years.

However, David was a different kind of man. Instead of focusing solely on his own enjoyment, he thought about the Ark of the Covenant, which was a symbol of God's presence back then. He realized that his own house was better than the location of the Ark. Considering the fact that the Ark symbolized God's presence, the king felt that the Ark deserved to be in a much better place, and he decided to do something about it.

To receive spiritual guidance, the king asked Prophet Nathan's opinion before taking any steps. That portion is what we have as the opening passage of this chapter. "Go, do all that is in thine heart; for the LORD is with thee" was the prophet's response. David now had the green light to undertake a major project in honor of God, and he could hardly wait to get started.

Before the king could start with the work, God sent a message to him through the same prophet:

"And it came to pass that night, that the word of the LORD came unto Nathan, saying, Go and tell my servant David, Thus saith the LORD, Shalt thou build me an house for me to dwell in? Whereas I have not dwelt in any house since the time that I brought up the children of Israel out of Egypt, even to this day, but have walked in a tent and in a tabernacle. In all the places wherein I have walked with all the children of Israel spake I a word with any of the tribes of Israel, whom I commanded to feed my people Israel, saying, Why build ye not me an house of cedar?" (2 Sam. 7:4–7).

The Lord made it clear that the Ark had always dwelt in a tent. He had never asked any of His servants to build a special house of cedar for the Ark. God's reaction shows that David's unprecedented desire to honor the Lord impressed God. The Lord recalled how He found David, anointed him to become king, protected him from the wishes of his enemies, and brought him this far. God felt pleased to see this man's great heart once again and decided to bless David even more. He promised building David a house.

"Now therefore so shalt thou say unto my servant David, Thus saith the LORD of hosts, I took thee from the sheepcote, from following the sheep, to be ruler over my people, over Israel: And I was with thee

whithersoever thou wentest, and have cut off all thine enemies out of thy sight, and have made thee a great name, like unto the name of the great men that are in the earth. Moreover I will appoint a place for my people Israel, and will plant them, that they may dwell in a place of their own, and move no more; neither shall the children of wickedness afflict them any more, as beforetime, And as since the time that I commanded judges to be over my people Israel, and have caused thee to rest from all thine enemies. Also the LORD telleth thee that he will make thee an house" (2 Sam. 7:8–11).

God pledged to bless the descendants of David and guaranteed that his children would continue to sit on the throne of Israel through an everlasting covenant. He also assured David that one of his sons would build the house that David had in mind:

"And when thy days be fulfilled, and thou shalt sleep with thy fathers, I will set up thy seed after thee, which shall proceed out of thy bowels, and I will establish his kingdom. He shall build an house for my name, and I will stablish the throne of his kingdom for ever. I will be his father, and he shall be my son. If he commit iniquity, I will chasten him with the rod of men, and with the stripes of the children of men: But my mercy shall not depart away from him, as I took it from Saul, whom I put away before thee. And thine house and thy kingdom shall be established for ever before thee: thy throne shall be established for ever" (2 Sam. 7:12–16).

God's kind words and promises melted David's tender heart. The king felt overwhelmed by God's mercy and faithfulness, and he began to thank and praise God. The humility of his heart before God and the attitude of gratitude kept him appreciating God increasingly. The king wondered why God was showing him so much kindness.

"Then went king David in, and sat before the LORD, and he said, Who am I, O Lord GOD? and what is my house, that thou hast brought me hitherto? And this was yet a small thing in thy sight, O Lord GOD; but thou hast spoken also of thy servant's house for a great while to come. And is this the manner of man, O Lord GOD? And what can David say more unto thee? for thou, Lord GOD, knowest thy servant. For thy word's sake, and according to thine own heart, hast thou done all these great things, to make thy servant know them. Wherefore thou art great, O LORD God: for there is none like thee, neither is there any God beside thee, according to all that we have heard with our ears" (2 Sam. 7:18–22).

David had heard about the Lord's greatness and had opportunities to experience this great God in his own personal life. He had a personal conviction of the goodness, the greatness, and the power of God, and his heart was fully set to please the Lord in every possible way. David remained a man after God's heart because he never stopped reflecting on God's faithfulness.

Take a moment to think about God's goodness in your own life, and you will feel a deep desire to praise Him and to do more things for His glory and for the prosperity of His kingdom. David once wrote:

"Bless the LORD, O my soul: and all that is within me, bless his holy name. Bless the LORD, O my soul, and forget not all his benefits: Who forgiveth all thine iniquities; who healeth all thy diseases; Who redeemeth thy life from destruction; who crowneth thee with lovingkindness and tender mercies; Who satisfieth thy mouth with good things; so that thy youth is renewed like the eagle's" (Ps. 103:1–5).

See God as God alone

Our mission in this life is to demonstrate to the world that the Lord our God is God above all other gods. It is our duty to let the world see that our God is merciful, kind, glorious, great, all powerful, and almighty. We can only present God to our world according to how we perceive and appreciate Him in our own hearts and lives. How do you see God?

David saw God as God and made up His mind to treat Him as such.

"Wherefore thou art great, O LORD God: for there is none like thee, neither is there any God beside thee, according to all that we have heard with our ears" (2 Sam. 7:22).

David's heart echoed the song of Moses after watching God deliver the Hebrews from bondage:

"Who is like unto thee, O LORD, among the gods? who is like thee, glorious in holiness, fearful in praises, doing wonder?" (Ex. 15:11).

God reveals His greatness to His people, not only to bless them but also to help them see and understand that He is God:

"Unto thee it was shewed, that thou mightiest know that the LORD he is God; there is none else beside him" (Deut. 4:35).

Hannah understood this truth firsthand after giving birth to Samuel, a son she had waited and prayed to have for several years. She had been barren for many years and had almost lost hope of getting a child when the Lord blessed her with a son. In her joy, she sang to the Lord, affirming Him as God:

"There is none holy as the LORD: for there is none beside thee: neither is there any rock like our God" (1 Sam. 2:2).

Micah saw God's compassion:

"Who is a God like unto thee, that pardoneth iniquity, and passeth by the transgression of the remnant of his heritage? He retaineth not his anger for ever, because he delighteth in mercy. He will turn again, he will have compassion upon us; he will subdue our iniquities; and thou wilt cast all their sins into the depths of the sea" (Micah 7:18–19).

Speaking of Himself, the Lord declares:

"I am the LORD, and there is none else, there is no God beside me: I girded thee, though thou hast not know me: That they may know from the rising of the sun, and from the west, that there is none beside me. I am the LORD, and there is none else. I form the light, and create darkness: I make peace, and create evil: I the LORD do all these things" (Isaiah 45:5–7).

"For thus saith the LORD that created the heavens; God himself that formed the earth and made it; he hath established it, he created it not in vain, he formed it to be inhabited: I am the LORD; and there is none else" (Is. 45:18).

"Look unto me, and be ye saved, and all the ends of the earth: for I am God, and there is none else" (Is. 45:22).

David saw the importance of having all nations worship this God: *"Among the gods there is none like unto thee, O Lord; neither are there any works like unto thy works. All nations whom thou hast made shall come and worship before thee, O Lord; and shall glorify thy name. For thou art great, and doest wondrous things: thou art God alone"* (Ps. 86:8–10).

When we experience God's goodness and greatness in our lives, we make the natural conclusion that He is God. Seeing Him as God makes us submit to Him and desire to see others come to the same conclusion about Him. This desire makes us want to push His agenda forward, and this agenda includes expanding His Kingdom by demonstrating His goodness and greatness in order for others to know Him and to serve Him as we do.

Live for the prosperity of God's Kingdom

A kingdom is the domain, territory, or realm in which a king rules. The Kingdom of God therefore refers to the rule of God. To prosper God's Kingdom means to expand the territories under His rule, to promote Him in all territories, and to help all people come to know Him and to submit to Him.

We can do this by living as role models, by preaching the Gospel, by financing kingdom-minded initiatives, by demonstrating God's power, and in many other ways.

One of the main reasons why God blesses His children with material prosperity is to make sure that they have the resources necessary to prosper His Kingdom in this world. Our hearts should be set to establish God's Kingdom. We have to make money and grow riches with a sense of mission, the mission to establish the Kingdom of God!
"But seek ye first the kingdom of God, and his righteousness; and all these things shall be added unto you" (Matt. 6:33).

"All these things" in the passage above refers to the material needs of life, such as food, clothing, shelter, and the things that we consider necessary in this world. The Lord Jesus wants us to give a higher priority to the Kingdom of God and all that is right for the Kingdom. In other words, we are to live kingdom-minded, kingdom-driven, and kingdom-centered lifestyles. We must be determined to do the right things according to God's purpose and will and to work with Him to advance His plans.

The advancement of God's work depends on the prosperity of God's people. God spreads His work by prospering His children.

"Cry yet, saying, Thus saith the LORD of hosts; My cities through prosperity shall yet be spread abroad; and the LORD shall yet comfort Zion, and shall yet choose Jerusalem" (Zec. 1:17).

Serve as God's channel for blessing the families of the earth

As we have seen earlier in this book, God promised His children *"a land flowing with milk and honey"* (Ex. 3:8), symbolizing a place of material blessings in abundance for them to represent Him, enjoy life, touch lives, leave an inheritance for their children's children, and to fulfill His part of the covenant with their fathers: Abraham, Isaac, and Jacob.

He gave them power to get wealth in order to bless the families of the earth through them as we can read from the Bible passages below:

"But thou shalt remember the LORD thy God: for it is he that giveth thee power to get wealth, that he may establish his covenant which he

sware unto thy fathers, as it is this day" (Deut. 8:18).

"And I will bless them that bless thee, and curse him that curseth thee: and in thee shall all families of the earth be blessed" (Gen. 12:3).

"And thy seed shall be as the dust of the earth, and thou shalt spread abroad to the west, and to the east, and to the north, and to the south: and in thee and in thy seed shall all the families of the earth be blessed" (Gen. 28:14).

"And I will make thy seed to multiply as the stars of heaven, and will give unto thy seed all these countries; and in thy seed shall all the nations of the earth be blessed; Because that Abraham obeyed my voice, and kept my charge, my commandments, my statutes, and my laws" (Gen. 26:4–5).

Abraham and his descendants received God's blessings because of their special relationship with God. He could call the Lord God his God. His children could do the same. This unique relationship was the secret of their success in God.

As the psalmist rightly puts it:

"Blessed is the man whom thou choosest, and causeth to approach unto thee, that he may dwell in thy courts: we shall be satisfied with the goodness of thy house, even of thy holy temple" (Ps. 65:4)

"Happy is he that hath the God of Jacob for his help, whose hope is in the LORD his God" (Ps. 146:5)

"Blessed is the nation whose God is the LORD; and the people whom he hath chosen for his own inheritance" (Ps. 33:12).

"Happy is that people, that is in such a case: yea, happy is that people, whose God is the LORD" (Ps. 144:15).

"For the LORD hath chosen Jacob unto himself, and Israel for his peculiar treasure" (Ps. 135:4).

"But thou, Israel, art my servant, Jacob whom I have chosen, the seed of Abraham my friend. Thou whom I have taken from the ends of the earth, and called thee from the chief men thereof, and said unto thee, Thou art my servant; I have chosen thee, and not cast thee away. Fear thou not; for I am with thee: be not dismayed; for I am thy God: I will strengthen thee; yea, I will help thee; yea, I will uphold thee with the right hand of my righteousness" (Is. 41:8–10).

Beyond the Jews

God had the greater world in mind when He called Abraham out of his country. Although God made the original promise of abundant blessings to Abraham and his descendants, or the Jews, the Gentiles, also referred to as the heathen or non-Jews, gained access to the blessings through the Lord Jesus Christ.

After the death and resurrection of the Lord Jesus Christ, the door opened for the entire world to experience this special relationship with God and to become part of God's family through faith.

"Christ hath redeemed us from the curse of the law, being made a curse for us: for it is written, Cursed is every one that hangeth on a tree: That the blessing of Abraham might come on the Gentiles through Jesus Christ; that we might receive the promise of the Spirit through faith" (Gal 3:13-14).

"For ye are all the children of God by faith in Christ Jesus. For as many of you as have been baptized into Christ have put on Christ. There is neither Jew nor Greek, there is neither bond nor free, there is neither male nor female: for ye are all one in Christ Jesus. And if ye be Christ's, then are ye Abraham's seed, and heirs according to the promise" (Gal. 3:26–29).

"Then took he him up in his arms, and blessed God, and said, Lord, now lettest thou thy servant depart in peace, according to thy word: For mine eyes have seen thy salvation, Which thou hast prepared before the face of all people; A light to lighten the Gentiles, and the glory of thy people Israel" (Luke 2:28–32).

"Wherefore remember, that ye being in time past Gentiles in the flesh, who are called Uncircumcision by that which is called the Circumcision in the flesh made by hands; That at that time ye were without Christ, being aliens from the commonwealth of Israel, and strangers from the covenants of promise, having no hope, and without God in the world: But now in Christ Jesus ye who sometimes were far off are made nigh by the blood of Christ. For he is our peace, who hath made both one, and hath broken down the middle wall of partition between us" (Eph. 2:11–14).

"And he said, It is a light thing that thou shouldest be my servant to raise up the tribes of Jacob, and to restore preserved of Israel: I will also give thee for a light to the Gentiles, that thou mayest be my salvation unto the end of the earth" (Is. 49:6).

The Gospel or *good news* is all about total salvation and access to God through Christ Jesus, our Lord. Through Him, those that are lost in darkness can now walk in the light. Those in sin can now receive forgiveness and live to touch other lives, whether they are Jews or Gentiles.

Our mission as believers is to take this Gospel to every person that is on the earth and to give every individual the opportunity to take part in God's blessings. This requires enormous financial resources, as we need to make use of the media, such as television, radio, newspapers, magazines, the Internet, and so on.

It also involves traveling, publishing, planting churches, establishing training centers, setting up community service centers, financing workers, and much more. Having material riches puts you in a position to serve as one of God's most reliable channels for blessings the families of the earth through the Gospel of our Lord Jesus Christ.

The eternal value of your material riches

People cannot take money, gold, houses, or any material riches with them when they depart from this world, but as strange as it may sound to some readers, we can affirm that money has eternal value!

Do you want to know how? It is quite simple: By making proper use of money, you can make it possible for people to spend eternity with God, thus making your material riches count in eternity. God wants you to use material riches with eternity in mind. To prosper His Kingdom, we must live our lives making conscious efforts to facilitate His eternal purpose for man.

As you enjoy the blessings of God in your personal life, look beyond your own needs, and strive to be rich in good works by meeting the material needs of the people around you. As you touch the people around you, think beyond your time and leave an inheritance for several generations of your heirs. As you consider the future of your descendants, think even beyond them, into eternity, and prosper the Kingdom of God through your material riches.

Find the right balance in all of these, and you will be on your way to a life of great fulfillment far beyond personal satisfaction. Learn to identify and use the best ways to prosper God's Kingdom in your time and beyond.

Ways to prosper God's Kingdom in our time

Here are some important ways you can advance the Kingdom of God in our time.

a) Invest in the local church

The church is the place where people meet for fellowship and receive godly education, spiritual nourishment, encouragement, motivation, love, direction, and general support. It is the place for believers to belong, to serve, and to be accountable. The Bible calls the church the "pillar and ground of the truth":

"But if I tarry long, that thou mayest know how thou oughtest to behave thyself in the house of God, which is the church of the living God, the pillar and ground of the truth" (1 Tim. 3:15).

Use money to pay for church expenses, fund expansion efforts, finance projects, and facilitate the accomplishment of God's mandate and the fulfillment of God's vision for the ministries in the church. Make sure that you have financial budget in place for your local church.

Many Christians do too little to support their churches. Some believers complain in services when preachers try to take up offerings. They accuse these preachers of paying too much attention to money. Make sure that you are not one of these complainers. Be proactive in rendering financial support to your local church.

While one may disagree with the methods some preachers use in taking up offerings, the true believer should rejoice with every new opportunity to make a financial contribution to worthy causes in the Kingdom of God. Do not waste your time trying to be the judge of God's servants. Simply listen to the heart of God, and obey Him with your finances, giving whenever He instructs you to do so.

Preachers do not necessarily enjoy taking up offerings or talking about money. They often feel forced to do so because of the need to finance God's work and because many believers in our churches today do not take the initiative to fund God's work. They focus more on their own needs and wait for preachers to call on them before they give.

Christians need to take responsibility for the operational costs of the house of God without waiting for anyone to ask them. Responsible people take the initiative to pay their utility bills, house rents, and other expenses regularly without being compelled, motivated, confronted, begged, or rebuked.

Church members tend to wait for pastors to pray, fast, and put new holes in their belt in the hope that someone in the congregation will hear God's voice and make some donations. This should not be necessary. The vast majority of the churchgoers visit the house of God to receive and not to give. As a result, they get upset when someone stands up front to talk about money. They take offense easily and look for reasons to justify their lack of willingness to take financial responsibility, whether such reasons are legitimate or not.

Angels in Heaven will not come down to clean our church buildings, and they will not pay our church electricity bills. God does not need to send cash down from the sky to pay the bills of the church. His intention is to prosper His work by prospering His children. Therefore, part of the riches that He gives to us have missions to accomplish in our local churches.

Look at your local church, and let the Lord speak to you. Does the church need new chairs? Is there a need to move to a new location? Is there a need to buy new musical instruments or to replace or upgrade the existing equipment? Does the interior need decoration? Are there other bills still open for the church to pay? Is your church involved in an important community service effort and in need of funding?

Speak to your church leaders to find out the best way to make financial contributions to the work, or simply send money to the church's bank account. Find out the needs and take the initiative to become part of the solution, and the Lord will continue to bless you with greater riches.

David took the initiative to build a house for God. Follow his good example. Do not wait for a long sermon from any preacher about giving before you carry out your financial responsibilities towards God's house.

Do everything within your power to make sure that God's house is worth connecting with God's name. Serve the house in the spirit of excellence, and God will increase His blessings in your life. God does not like to see His children neglect His house:

"Thus speaketh the LORD of hosts, saying, This people say, The time is not come, the time that the LORD'S house should be built. Then came the word of the LORD by Haggai the prophet, saying, Is it time for you, O ye, to dwell in your cieled houses, and this house lie waste? Now therefore thus saith the LORD of hosts; Consider your ways. Ye have sown much, and bring in little; ye eat, but ye have not enough; ye drink, but ye are not filled with drink; ye clothe you, but there is none warm; and he that earneth wages earneth wages to put it into a bag with holes. Thus saith the LORD of hosts; Consider your ways. Go up to the mountain, and bring wood, and build the house; and I will take pleasure in it, and I will be glorified, saith the LORD" (Hag. 1:2–8).

Taking care of God's house helps to reveal God's glory. His glory attracts the people in the world and opens the door for their salvation and the prosperity of His Kingdom.

There is a strong connection between the condition of God's house and the advancement of God's purpose. God's purpose prospers when God's people pay attention to everything that reflects on God's glory and do whatever it takes to lift up the name of the Lord Jesus. The opposite is also true. God's purpose suffers when God's children are careless about His glory and His name and settle for lower standards. Does your local church feel the impact of God's material blessings in your life? Are you a faithful member? Are you making any significant difference? If not, then you can decide to change from this point.

b) *Support ministers of the Gospel*

Many preachers dedicate their lives to the progress of God's people only to end up forgotten by the very people they have served with the most important parts of their lives. Apart from the neglect that they suffer, many of them come under strong criticism and opposition of unimaginable proportions. They are often subjects of gossip, backstabbing, and ridicule, and they suffer pain at the hands of those that they love. This is unfortunate because God intended to have His people take care of His servants.

"Let him that is taught in the word communicate unto him that teacheth in all good things"
(Gal. 6:6).

"Take heed to thyself that thou forsake not the Levite as long as thou livest upon the earth" (Deut. 12:19).

"If we have sown unto you spiritual things, is it a great thing if we shall reap your carnal things?"
(1 Cor. 9:11).

"For it hath pleased them of Macedonia and Achaia to make a certain contribution for the poor saints which are at Jerusalem. It hath pleased them verily; and their debtors they are. For if the Gentiles have been made partakers of their spiritual things, their duty is also to minister unto them in carnal things" (Rom. 15:26–27).

It is not appropriate for a person to minister spiritual blessings to people and not partake in their material blessings. It goes against God's principle for people to prosper under the leadership of a servant of God and not make conscious efforts to ensure the material prosperity of such a minister. To walk in the fullness of God's blessings, God's people must follow God's principles *fully*.

Develop the habit of releasing material blessings into the lives of every man or woman of God that the Lord sends your way. They carry God's blessings with them, and you will not miss your reward if you honor them. Remember the words of our Lord Jesus Christ:

"For whosoever shall give you a cup of water to drink in my name, because ye belong to Christ, verily I say unto you, he shall not lose his reward" (Mark 9:41).

"He that receiveth a prophet in the name of a prophet shall receive a prophet's reward; and he that receiveth a righteous man in the name of a righteous man shall receive a righteous man's reward" (Matt. 10:41).

It is not possible to prosper the Kingdom of God fully without paying attention to the material needs of those that consistently labor for the advancement of the Kingdom. While church buildings are important, they cannot take the place of God's servants.

Many ministers of the Gospel suffer material lack today, not because God has not provided for them but because the people that God chose to use as channels to bless His servants often end up ignoring God's instructions and following their own agendas. You must never use for a different purpose that which God intends for you to use for blessing His servants. That would be robbery and misappropriation of funds, a sin in the eyes of God! Remain faithful, and supply the needs of God's servants as the Lord commands.

Meditate on the passage below:

"Who then is a faithful and wise servant, whom his lord hath made ruler over his household, to give them meat in due season? Blessed is that servant, whom his lord when he cometh shall find so doing. Verily I say unto you, That he shall make him ruler over all his goods. But and if that evil servant shall say in his heart, My lord delayeth his coming; And shall begin to smite his fellowservants, and to eat and drink with the drunken; The lord of that servant shall come in a day when he looketh not for him, and in an hour that he is not aware of, And shall cut him asunder, and appoint him his portion with the hypocrites: there shall be weeping and gnashing of teeth" (Matt. 24:45–51).

Although many church leaders have suffered abuse at the hands of church members, there are great examples of believers all over the world that understand the importance of honoring God's servants and showing appreciation for their commitment to the work of God.

Some of these believers build houses for their pastors, buy them cars, finance their trips, pay for the education of their children, arrange household help for them, and do everything possible to make sure that they have no reasons to worry about personal material or earthly needs. These believers make it possible for such ministers to focus on spiritual matters.

It eventually benefits the people of God and the Kingdom of God because preachers are at their best when they can focus on spiritual matters. The work of God and the people of God thrive in such places where God's people make it possible for spiritual leaders to focus on the spiritual aspects of God's work.

Some people feel comfortable seeing preachers live in material lack and poverty because they think that such conditions keep them humble and draw them closer to God. Such people reject the idea of preachers receiving a high income and living comfortably, but the Bible teaches us otherwise.

"Let the elders that rule well be counted worthy of double honour, especially they who labour in the word and doctrine. For the scripture saith, Thou shalt not muzzle the ox that treadeth out the corn. And, The labourer is worthy of his reward" (1 Tim. 5:17–18).

God does not only expect His servants to have material reward for their labor, He actually considers them worthy of double honor! Learn to consider it perfectly fine for God's servants to have more than their personal financial and material needs. Work together with the Lord to be one of the people that will make it possible.

c) *Finance the spread of the Gospel:*

To advance the Kingdom of God, we must spread the Gospel and lead more people to the Lord. This is an important part of our purpose here in this world.

"And Jesus came and spake unto them, saying, All power is given unto me in heaven and in earth. Go ye therefore, and teach all nations, baptizing them in the name of the Father, and of the Son, and of the Holy Ghost: Teaching them to observe all things whatsoever I have commanded you: and, lo, I am with you alway, even unto the end of the world. Amen" (Matt. 28:18–20).

"And he said unto them, Go ye into all the world, and preach the gospel to every creature. He that believeth and is baptized shall be saved; but he that believeth not shall be damned. And these signs shall follow them that believe; In my name shall they cast out devils;

they shall speak with new tongues; They shall take up serpents; and if they drink any deadly thing, it shall not hurt them; they shall lay hands on the sick, and they shall recover" (Mark 16:15–18).

"Ye have not chosen me, but I have chosen you, and ordained you, that ye should go and bring forth fruit, and that your fruit should remain: that whatsoever ye shall ask of the Father in my name, he may give it you" (John 15:16).

The commandment to go out and evangelize the world is what many Bible scholars call "The Great Commission." This commandment shows us that God wants to see people saved.

"I exhort therefore, that, first of all, supplications, prayers, intercessions, and giving of thanks, be made for all men; For kings, and for all that are in authority; that we may lead a quiet and peaceable life in all godliness and honesty. For this is good and acceptable in the sight of God our Saviour; Who will have all men to be saved, and to come unto the knowledge of the truth" (1 Tim. 2:1–4).

"The Lord is not slack concerning his promise, as some men count slackness; but is longsuffering to us-ward, not willing that any should perish, but that all should come to repentance" (2 Pet. 3:9).

"For I have no pleasure in the death of him that dieth, saith the Lord GOD: wherefore turn yourselves, and live ye" (Ezek. 18:32).

"For God so loved the world, that he gave his only begotten Son, that whosoever believeth in him should not perish, but have everlasting life. For God sent not his Son into the world to condemn the world; but that the world through him might be saved" (John 3:16–17).

Knowing that God wants people to experience salvation, we must do everything within our power to make use of the resources within our disposal to make this happen. Your money can take the Gospel to places where you have no time, intention, or opportunity to go in person. Give eternal value to your material riches by sponsoring Gospel initiatives. God considers souls important, and so must you!

"For what shall it profit a man, if he shall gain the whole world, and lose his own soul? Or what shall a man give in exchange for his soul?" (Mark 8:36–37).

Use your money to make angels celebrate in Heaven each time a sinner turns to the Lord:

"I say unto you, that likewise joy shall be in heaven over one sinner that repenteth, more than over ninety and nine just persons, which need no repentance" (Luke 15:7).

Is it not exciting to know that you can cause celebration in Heaven with your money here on earth? As you can see, money is not only good for this world. You can use money to stir up celebration in Heaven and to change how people on earth will spend eternity if you make use of money in the right way. Being rich is a good thing and a great privilege, a blessing from God that we must use for His eternal purpose.

You make the world a better place each time that you lead a sinner to the Lord. When a potential rapist comes to God, potential victims are safer. The Bible says that we prevent evils by converting people.

"Brethren, if any of you do err from the truth, and one convert him;

Let him know, that he which converteth the sinner from the error of his way shall save a soul from death, and shall hide a multitude of sins" (James 5:19–20).

We prosper the Kingdom of God by converting people to the Lord and by training them to walk in the ways of the Lord. Do you have a strategic plan and a sustainable budget for winning souls into the Kingdom? You should! Are you taking conscious steps in order to make sure that the Gospel reaches places where people have never heard the name of the Lord Jesus? You should! If not, take some time to pray and ask the Lord to direct you about how to touch more lives with His material blessings in your life.

d) Support strategic Kingdom advancement initiatives:

In addition to financing the spread of the Gospel, make money available to support other Kingdom advancement initiatives, such as conferences, seminars, workshops, Bible schools, media acquisitions, and a host of other strategic and fruitful efforts geared towards the prosperity of God's kingdom, and the Lord will continue to prosper you.

e) Remember ministry efforts when you write your will:

Another possible way to prosper the Kingdom of God beyond your lifetime is to remember God's work when you write your will. Consult with the Lord to find out if He will permit you to leave a portion for a local church, a distant ministry, a preacher, a project, or anything that may prosper His work.

Make your money and wealth touch lives beyond you and meet needs beyond your personal necessities. Serve God's eternal purpose with your earthly riches. God left you in this world to affect history for His glory. Do not settle for anything less than His highest plans for you.

10

CREATE WEALTH WITH A SENSE OF DIVINE PURPOSE

"And the king made silver and gold at Jerusalem as plenteous as stones, and cedar trees made he as the sycomore trees that are in the vale for abundance" (2 Chron. 1:15).

Do not just create wealth for the sake of becoming rich. Build wealth with a sense of divine purpose.

The king referred to in the opening passage above is King Solomon. He was the richest king in the Bible. Solomon was also one of the most fortunate kings in the Bible. King David, Solomon's father, gave him spiritual instructions and left him with a great estate and material wealth before his death. God also blessed Solomon with additional riches and gave him favor with other leaders in his time. Kings sent him supplies from different parts of the world, and Solomon had far more riches than he needed in a lifetime.

He was not the only one who was prosperous. His prosperity affected the condition of the land as well. With time, the land had gold in abundance. As you can read from the passage above, the king filled Jerusalem with an abundance of silver and gold as if they were mere stones. Solomon established Jerusalem as a tourist center, and the rest of the world admired and feared the Jews for the power of their God, for the prosperity in the land, and for the wisdom of King Solomon. Jerusalem became a place of prayer and a major business hub during his reign.

The land enjoyed great peace and prosperity and began to draw the rest of the world closer to God, on track to becoming God's channel of blessings to the families of the earth, but the king had a weakness! He loved many strange women, most of whom were idol worshippers. In his old age, these women turned his heart away from God, provoking God to anger. Consequently, the land missed a good chance to continue serving as a role model to the rest of the world.

King Solomon had wisdom, knowledge, riches, wealth, and honor. He started with the fear of the Lord and had a great zeal to lead God's people in God's will, but he ended up poorly because he did not overcome his weakness for women early enough in his life. Solomon's failure in this single area of his life became a major hindrance to the overall purpose of God for blessing him. This goes to show that the weaknesses that people do not overcome eventually overcome them.

Unfortunately, people with great potentials never fall alone! Their potential makes them influential, and others usually fall along with them. The fall of Solomon tainted the history of the land and had adverse effects on the entire nation and the purpose that God had in mind for His people and for the rest of the world.

Keep the purpose in mind

Riches and wealth are perfectly fine, and every child of God should have them in abundance. However, they are only important for the reasons that God wants us to have them, and the power of money is only good if we make use of that power to fulfill God's purpose. As we have seen earlier, there are five main reasons why God blesses His people with material riches:

- ✓ To serve as **ambassadors**
- ✓ For their **enjoyment**
- ✓ To make them rich in **good works**
- ✓ For them to leave an **inheritance** for generations to come
- ✓ To make them prosper **His Kingdom**

Ultimately, our riches should become tools for blessing the families of the earth. They should serve as weapons against poverty, destitution, pain, and everything that our God wants to eradicate from our world. Riches should position us to have positive influence in our societies and ensure that people in our world are heading towards eternity with God. Solomon built a great temple, a place for people to worship the true God, but he personally neglected the importance of staying away from idols.

Many people, including Christians, are pursuing wealth today without God's purpose in mind. They simply want to have material riches, and they do not seem to mind if they ignore God's instructions in the process. They tend to ignore His promptings and warnings against ungodly ways for making money and hope that they can just repent after becoming rich.

They trade their righteousness for material riches because God's approach appears too difficult to them, and His methods appear too slow for the pace of progress that they envision. Do not fall into the trap with them!

It is better to have little and live in the fear of God than to have abundance and fall from grace. However, it is possible for you to have both. You can be pure and rich at the same time. Go for all that God intends for your life. "All" includes purity, spiritual power, wisdom, material riches, and everything else that the Bible promises to God's people.

Do not neglect or reject any of His great and precious promises. Follow the Bible's injunction for us to grow in grace:

"Grace and peace be multiplied unto you through the knowledge of God, and of Jesus our Lord, According as his divine power hath given unto us all things that pertain unto life and godliness, through the knowledge of him that hath called us to glory and virtue: Whereby are given unto us exceeding great and precious promises: that by these ye might be partakers of the divine nature, having escaped the corruption that is in the world through lust. And beside this, giving all diligence, add to your faith virtue; and to virtue knowledge; And to knowledge temperance; and to temperance patience; and to patience godliness; And to godliness brotherly kindness; and to brotherly kindness charity. For if these things be in you, and abound, they make you that ye shall neither be barren nor unfruitful in the knowledge of our Lord Jesus Christ" (2 Pet. 1:2–8).

"But grow in grace, and in the knowledge of our Lord and Saviour Jesus Christ. To him be glory both now and for ever. Amen" (2 Pet. 3:18).

Study the Bible. Obey what you read. Learn to know the Lord more, and walk in His ways.

Excel in your field

To reach greater heights in life, identify the special gifts and talents of God in your life, and excel in them. Get the training that you need, and then work with dedication to excel in the fields. Do everything within your God-given ability to lead your field. God wants you to be the head and not the tail. He wants you to be the first and not the last. He wants you to be above *only*!

Learn to recognize the special qualities of God in your life. Appreciate the talents, and celebrate your uniqueness. Do not strive to be anyone else. The less you try to be like others, the more likely you are to discover new qualities in your own life.

Cain was a farmer. Abel had his way with animals. Noah was an architect and a builder. Abraham was a shepherd. Esau was a man of the field. Jacob was a homebody. Aaron was a good speaker, and Miriam was a composer and a singer. You definitely have qualities in you.

Bezaleel's special abilities made him creative with gold, silver, and brass (Ex. 31:1–5). Aholib had special talents for making furniture, candlesticks, special garments, and so on (Ex. 31:6–10). The children of Issachar had special discernment for times and seasons, making it possible for them to give timely directions to the children of Israel (1 Chron. 12:32).

Solomon had wisdom and was able to serve as a consultant to kings and queens of other nations. Joseph, the husband of Mary, the mother of our Lord Jesus, was a carpenter. Peter was an angler. Paul made tents (Acts 18:13).

You are likely to have one, two, three, or more talents in your own life. Learn, practice, master, and excel in what you do!

Attend seminars, read books, follow courses, and do whatever it takes to continue learning and growing. There are more learning opportunities in our time than there has been at any other time in history. Take advantage of the Internet, and upgrade your current level of education.

Take time to meditate and receive new inspirations for creative innovations. Our God has many new ideas that He wants to release to the earth. Make yourself available to Him through special times of prayer and meditation, and you will never be short of crucial revelations in our increasingly competitive world.

There are divine ideas waiting for God's people to discover, and you can download them for your world if you take the time to think along with God. Make time to think!

Stir up the gifts of God in your life, and take your performance to a new, higher level. Develop the habit of beating your own record each time, and do not settle for anything less than the best of God for your life. After doing your best, strive for something higher and greater!

Monetize your craft

God's talents in our lives are there to help us survive, succeed, excel in this world, and touch lives so that we can serve His purpose. The talents contain His sources of income and the tools that you need for fulfilling the ministry and His calling on your life. Therefore, they should help you to make money and position you to serve God's purpose more effectively. Your livelihood and prosperity depend on how you leverage the gifts of God in your life. Your gifts should be increasing your material riches. If not, you need to re-examine how you are currently making use of them.

Many people with potential for great material prosperity are living in poverty because they do not leverage their talents and gifts properly. You may have seen people use for charity the seeds designed for trade, ending up with lack, begging others for help, and constantly needing miracles to survive!

Some believers open stores for business only to close after a short period because they take a charity approach to business, giving out free items to people and "believing God" to provide! They then go through a period of lack and call on the Lord for help only for them to start and fold up again. Their misplaced desire to help people often end up becoming the greatest hindrances to the prosperity that God wants to see in their lives.

The natural heart of compassion that believers receive when they come to know the Lord makes it difficult for many of them to know how to separate business from charity. They want to be able to give precious things to people free.

To progress financially in order to fulfill God's purpose, every believer must know how to make money, grow money, manage money, and distribute money. It is important to know when a business is ready to start giving out money for charity and to know how much money to give at each phase. Doing so prematurely can cripple the business and defeat the purpose of touching lives.

It is beyond the scope of this book to go deeper into the subject of giving and receiving, growing business, and so on. However, it is essential to point out that we must learn how to monetize our talents and understand the language and principles of trade if we want to grow richer.

Paul the Apostle preached the Gospel without charge but charged people for the tents he built. No ruler went empty-handed to Solomon for counseling. Solomon and the land received material benefits from the wisdom that God gave to Solomon. God chose the Levites to serve in the temple and made sure that they had an abundance of provisions. A tithe of the income of the people went to them, placing them among the richest people in the land.

Think about a group of people receiving ten percent of the income of a prosperous nation and you will be able to imagine how rich the Levites were. The high priest, Aaron, received a tithe of the income of the Levites. That potentially made him one of the richest people in the land. He had supplies beyond his own need and was often able to take care of widows, orphans, strangers, and other vulnerable people in the land. God likes to see people benefit from everything that they do for Him and for others. As we have seen earlier in this book, our God rewards!

Do not give away for free that which the Lord intends to serve as your craft for generating wealth. Learn how to turn talents into financial treasures. Turn your passions into possessions, and use the profit to grow wealth and fulfill God's purpose. You may then use the income or the profit to touch lives and to do whatever the Lord would have you do. Paul understood the difference between free preaching and marketable tent constructions.

Most things in this life are not free. Even when they appear free, they are "free" because a person or a group of persons paid the price for them. If you choose to be the person paying that price, then you need to have one or more sources generating you income in order for you to be able to continue paying the price. If not, you will arrive at a place where you are depending on the generosity of others and their obedience to God for you to continue paying the price.

Every charity or "non-profit" work must be sustainable. We can reduce the amount of time we spend trying to get sponsors if we take more time to look into the possibilities of monetizing some of our potential and making our plans more sustainable. There must be a cycle of giving and receiving. Those watering others need watering as well (Prov. 11:25).

Examine everything that you do, and ask yourself the question, "How can I turn my craft into more cash and do more for the Kingdom?" Paul turned his craft of tent making into cash and used the money to take care of himself and those around him (Acts 20:33–35, Acts 18:1–3).

This allowed him to preach the Gospel without charge and to take responsibility for his own welfare, especially in places where he felt that people might misunderstand his motive for preaching. Although he had rights to receive material support from those that received spiritual support from him, he was able to set aside his rights in some places, partly because of his ability to monetize his craft.

Preachers should be able to receive income without needing to work outside of the church, but there is nothing wrong with them making money with other talents in their lives if they are able to combine their efforts without hindering their effectiveness in the various areas of their spiritual responsibilities.

As mentioned earlier, attend seminars, read books, take online classes, and do whatever is necessary to learn and excel in business thinking. Master the science and the art of using your God-given advantages, and monetize your potential. Generate money, and build wealth in abundance so that you can continue serving the Lord's purpose without delays and unnecessary financial limitations and distractions.

God wants you to make gain with the talents in your life. Do not hide them because of shyness, fear of failure, insecurity, or fear of persecution. Develop your entrepreneurial spirit. Learn about negotiation, sales, branding, publicity, networking, partnership, and other important subjects that can help you to do more with the gifts of God in your life. Renew your commitment towards material prosperity now!

Master the power of true commitment

Joseph and Mary, the parents of the Lord Jesus, like most Jewish families, travelled yearly to Jerusalem to take part in the Passover. During one of those trips, when the Lord Jesus was only twelve years old, they discovered on their way back to Nazareth, their hometown, that He was not with the rest of the family.

Determined to find him, they returned to Jerusalem to look for Him. Their long search ended when they found Him in the temple, in serious talks with the doctors of the law on subjects of the Scriptures.

The search meant that they would get home at least two days later than scheduled, and the mother took it a bit personally! *"... Son, why hast thou thus dealt with us? Behold, thy father and I have sought thee sorrowing"* (Luke 2:48).

His answer was unapologetic:

"And he said unto them, How is it that ye sought me? wist ye not that I must be about my Father's business?" (Luke 2:49).

With that response, He was trying to say that the place of the "Father's business" was the right place to look for Him. They could have avoided unnecessary headache by going to the right place the first time!

The Lord Jesus knew from an early age the plan of the Father for His life and had a clear determination to pursue and to perform all that God intended for Him.

He was committed to the fulfillment of God's mandate on His life, and this led to a highly successful life and an eternal legacy for the world. The Lord Jesus demonstrated the power of God, glorified the Father, prospered God's Kingdom, and changed human history!

People often succeed or fail according to their levels of commitment. Higher goals require greater commitment because great dreams attract great oppositions and challenges, and it takes strong dedication to press forward in the midst of serious opposition. Are you truly committed to wealth creation?

To commit oneself to something means to give in, to tie oneself to it, and to make a strong and determined promise to do what is necessary for the goal that one has in mind. A committed person takes promises seriously and does not look for flimsy excuses to withdraw from a cause.

Commitment ties us to our words and "forces" us to get things done. Every worthy goal requires one to pay the necessary price. Therefore, no one can accomplish great goals without true commitment. Building wealth in line with God's purpose requires strong commitment in several areas, including time, principles, wisdom, learning, hard work, prayers, networking, planning, personal discipline, humility, progress, and so many other areas.

Make up your mind to follow the preacher's instruction!

"Whatsoever thy hand findeth to do, do it with thy might; for there is no work, nor device, nor knowledge, nor wisdom, in the grave, whither thou goest" (Ecc. 9:10).

Live your life to the full

"For I am now ready to be offered, and the time of my departure is at hand. I have fought a good fight, I have finished my course, I have kept the faith: Henceforth there is laid up for me a crown of righteousness, which the Lord, the righteous judge, shall give me at that day: and not to me only, but unto all them also that love his appearing" (2 Tim. 4:6–8).

Paul the Apostle's life is an example of how to live life to the fullest. Reflecting on his fruitful walk with God, Paul, in his old age, wrote with confidence that he had fought a good fight, finished his course, and kept the faith. He was also sure of God's eternal reward, a crown of righteousness waiting for him.

Many people, on their deathbeds, take the time to examine their lives. They think about their successes and achievements. They also think about the things they could have done but failed to do, the words they could have spoken but did not speak. They think about the places they would have visited but did not visit. They consider the money they could have made but did not make and wish they could begin their lives or a part of their lives all over again! To such people, life passed too fast, and potential was wasted. They did not live their lives to the full!

God wants you to live a fulfilled life so that you can look back at the end of your time here on the earth with a sense of gratitude and appreciation for a life well spent. God wants you to be able to look back at your life, like Paul the Apostle, with a sense of satisfaction. You can do this by yielding to His will in all areas of your life.

While God has promised us abundance and prosperity in all areas, the road to abundant living can be rough, and the journey can be tough. There may be many raging storms along the way, and greatness is certainly not for the faint-hearted. Yet in all of the challenges, He has promised to be with you.

Therefore, make up your mind to live your life to the full. Decide to be strong, to be holy, to be rich, to be fruitful, to be confident, to be bold, to be humble, and to be all that He wants you to be so that you can do all that He wants you to do. Develop and live up to your full potential in Him so that you can rejoice at the end of your time in this world.

Paul had a great sense of fulfillment about his life as he approached the end of his time here on the earth. Such a feeling is beyond what most people consider success. It is true fulfillment.

Let us take a closer look at three phrases from the passage to get a better understanding of his experience:

1. "I have fought a good fight"

The word "good" in the phrase also means worthy or valuable. The word "fight" there means to strive or to labor fervently. Paul spent his life traveling around the then known world, reasoning with the wise and the simple, turning people from darkness to light and from the power of Satan to the power of God, making sure that widows and orphans received their necessary care, and changing the eternal direction of everyone that submitted to his message.

When possible, Paul also did business, as you can read from his own words:

"I have coveted no man's silver, or gold, or apparel. Yea, ye yourselves know, that these hands have ministered unto my necessities, and to them that were with me. I have shewed you all things, how that so labouring ye ought to support the weak, and to remember the words of the Lord Jesus, how he said, It is more blessed to give than to receive" (Acts 20:33–35).

"After these things Paul departed from Athens, and came to Corinth; And found a certain Jew named Aquila, born in Pontus, lately come

from Italy, with his wife Priscilla; (because that Claudius had commanded all Jews to depart from Rome:) and came unto them. And because he was of the same craft, he abode with them, and wrought: for by their occupation they were tentmakers" (Acts 18:1–3).

He went through persecution, suspicion, rejection, opposition, and many challenges. He worked and suffered under false workers but held his ground! He fought the good fight indeed. Paul experienced honor and dishonor. Yet in some of the most difficult times of his life, he made people rich! He labored fervently and made full use of the grace of God on his life.

"Are they ministers of Christ? (I speak as a fool) I am more; in labours more abundant, in stripes above measure, in prisons more frequent, in deaths oft. Of the Jews five times received I forty stripes save one. Thrice was I beaten with rods, once was I stoned, thrice I suffered shipwreck, a night and a day I have been in the deep; In journeyings often, in perils of waters, in perils of robbers, in perils by mine own countrymen, in perils by the heathen, in perils in the city, in perils in the wilderness, in perils in the sea, in perils among false brethren; In weariness and painfulness, in watchings often, in hunger and thirst, in fastings often, in cold and nakedness. Beside those things that are without, that which cometh upon me daily, the care of all the churches" (2 Cor. 11:23–28).

"But in all things approving ourselves as the ministers of God, in much patience, in afflictions, in necessities, in distresses, In stripes, in imprisonments, in tumults, in labours, in watchings, in fastings; By pureness, by knowledge, by long suffering, by kindness, by the Holy Ghost, by love unfeigned, By the word of truth, by the power of God, by the armour of righteousness on the right hand and on the left, By honor and dishonour, by evil report and good report: as deceivers,

and yet true; As unknown, and yet well known; as dying, and, behold, we live; as chastened, and not killed; As sorrowful, yet alway rejoicing; as poor, yet making many rich; as having nothing, and yet possessing all things" (2 Cor. 6:4–10).

"For I am the least of the apostles, that am not meet to be called an apostle, because I persecuted the church of God. But by the grace of God I am what I am: and his grace which was bestowed upon me was not in vain; but I laboured more abundantly than they all: yet not I, but the grace of God which was with me" (1 Cor. 15:9–10).

Remain consistent in your determination to fulfill God's plans for your material riches, and you will overcome every challenge on your path by His grace.

2. *"I have finished my course"*

The word "course" here also means career. To finish as used here means to reach the maximum level or the end of a thing. It is getting to the place where one has done *all* that there is to do in a thing. It is like studying to the highest academic level in a field or reaching the highest position possible within an organization. In the context of the passage, Paul was saying that he had already done his part of God's mandate on his life. How far are you willing to go in your determination to please God?

The Lord Jesus said something similar when He hung on the cross:

"After this, Jesus knowing that all things were now accomplished, that the scripture might be fulfilled, saith, I thirst. Now there was set a vessel full of vinegar: and they filled a spunge with vinegar, and put it upon hyssop, and put it to his mouth. When Jesus therefore had

received the vinegar, he said, It is finished: and he bowed his head, and gave up the ghost" (John 19:28–30).

It is a feeling of accomplishment to say *"It is finished."*

Are you committed to doing all that God wants you to do in this life? Will you generate all of the money that you can generate by His grace? Are you willing to build wealth for the fulfillment of His purpose? Do not settle for anything less!

3. *"I have kept the faith"*

To keep here means to guard diligently. In this context, it also means to *abide by* or to *adhere to* the standard. The word "faith" also means moral conviction, persuasion, principle, or belief. Paul walked in his spiritual convictions, followed the principles of the word of God, and lived in line with his moral persuasions. He held on to the truth with a strong determination to live it.

Consider the following passages of the Scriptures, and do the same thing:

"Buy the truth, and sell it not; also wisdom, and instruction, and understanding" (Prov. 23:23).

"But that on the good ground are they, which in an honest and good heart, having heard the word, keep it, and bring forth fruit with patience" (Luke 8:15).

"I know thy works: behold, I have set before thee an open door, and no man can shut it: for thou hast a little strength, and hast kept my word, and hast not denied my name" (Rev. 3:8).

"That good thing which was committed unto thee keep by the Holy Ghost which dwelleth in us"
(2 Tim. 1:14).

Walk by these principles as you reach out to achieve greater heights in God. Anyone wishing to be rich without following strong moral principles runs the great risk of corruption, falling from the faith, becoming materialistic, and ending up as a slave to money.

God wants you to be different from the vast majority of people pursuing money aimlessly. Therefore, it is extremely important that you adhere to God's rules. Walk in all honesty and in the fear of God. Rob no one. Cheat no one. Live with a conscience free of offense towards God and towards men.

"And herein do I exercise myself, to have always a conscience void of offence toward God, and toward men" (Acts 24:16).

Keep a clean conscience, and remember the importance of a good name:

"A good name is rather to be chosen than great riches, and loving favour rather than silver and gold" (Prov. 22:1).

Get closer to God as you become richer. As you become greater in your world, learn to humble yourself in the sight of the Lord so that He will never find it necessary to humble you!

Remember the Lord's faithfulness, and remain faithful

Remember His testimonies, and meditate on His goodness. You must never forget how His grace sustained you in all of the most difficult times of your journey. Remain thankful, and give Him the glory.

David is an example of thankfulness:

"Bless the LORD, O my soul: and all that is within me, bless his holy name. Bless the LORD, O my soul, and forget not all his benefits: Who forgiveth all thine iniquities; who healeth all thy diseases; Who redeemeth thy life from destruction; who crowneth thee with lovingkindness and tender mercies; Who satisfieth thy mouth with good things; so that thy youth is renewed like the eagle's" (Ps. 103:1–5).

"If it had not been the LORD who was on our side, now may Israel say; If it had not been the LORD who was on our side, when men rose up against us: Then they had swallowed us up quick, when their wrath was kindled against us: Then the waters had overwhelmed us, the stream had gone over our soul: Then the proud waters had gone over our soul. Blessed be the LORD, who hath not given us as a prey to their teeth. Our soul is escaped as a bird out of the snare of the fowlers: the snare is broken, and we are escaped. Our help is in the name of the LORD, who made heaven and earth" (Ps. 124:1–8).

Many people begin well and then fall after tasting success. God wants you to stay on track. He wants your light to shine brighter so that you can attract others to Him. Learn from the mistakes of the children of Israel.

Read the following Bible passage:

"For the LORD's portion is his people; Jacob is the lot of his inheritance. He found him in a desert land, and in the waste howling wilderness; he led him about, he instructed him, he kept him

as the apple of his eye. As an eagle stirreth up her nest, fluttereth over her young, spreadeth abroad her wings, taketh them, beareth them on her wings: So the LORD alone did lead him, and there was no strange god with him. He made him ride on the high places of the earth, that he might eat the increase of the fields; and he made him to suck honey out of the rock, and oil out of the flinty rock; Butter of kine, and milk of sheep, with fat of lambs, and rams of the breed of Bashan, and goats, with the fat of kidneys of wheat; and thou didst drink the pure blood of the grape. But Jeshurun waxed fat, and kicked: thou art waxen fat, thou art grown thick, thou art covered with fatness; then he forsook God which made him, and lightly esteemed the Rock of his salvation" (Deut. 32:9–15).

As you can read, God loved and promoted them, but they disappointed Him after tasting abundance. They forgot the purpose of the material riches in their lives and provoked God by serving idols!

"They provoked him to jealousy with strange gods, with abominations provoked they him to anger. They sacrificed unto devils, not to God; to gods whom they knew not, to new gods that came newly up, whom your fathers feared not. Of the Rock that begat thee thou art unmindful, and hast forgotten God that formed thee. And when the LORD saw it, he abhorred them, because of the provoking of his sons, and of his daughters. And he said, I will hide my face from them, I will see what their end shall be: for they are a very froward generation, children in whom is no faith" (Deut. 32:16–20).

Some people have the tendency to go closer to God when they are going through tough times only to forget Him when they are doing well. Others tend to serve God when things are going well only to abandon Him and seek their own ways when going through tough times. The true believer needs to be consistently

212

committed, serving the Lord fervently in all seasons and in every situation.

Rule over your riches! Money is powerful and must have a boss. Those that do not rule over money eventually end up becoming servants of money. Be the boss of the money in your hands, and let it serve God's plans.

As we have seen, God wants you to be rich, not just for the sake of riches but also for His greater purpose. Therefore, when He multiplies wealth in your hands, put your trust in Him and not in the abundance of the material things in your life.

When you "arrive," remember where you were when God found you, and behave yourself! Live to please Him, and remember the people that He used to help you along the way. Enjoy your life and walk in boldness, but do not lose the fear of the Lord!

Money is powerful, but do not trust your riches. Do not oppress people with your riches. Treat human beings with a sense of dignity and respect. Put your trust in the Lord!

"Trust not in oppression, and become not vain in robbery: if riches increase, set not your heart upon them" (Ps. 62:10).

Have you already started the journey?

Congratulations on coming this far! If you have not yet started the journey towards abundant material riches, then this is a good moment to ask God prayerfully for direction about the next steps that you must take towards creating wealth for His glory.

God is recruiting and raising a new generation of entrepreneurs today for the advancement of His Kingdom in our time. Will you join this movement?

If you have already started the journey, then continue with a stronger determination to generate more wealth for His glory!

Take someone with you on this exciting journey as you do more with passion, serve as God's representative, enjoy life, touch lives, leave an inheritance for generations, and prosper the Kingdom of God beyond your time.

Let us know how we can help you in your determination to learn, grow, and do more for the Kingdom of God. Our ministry loves to hear from our readers. Let us know if this book has been a blessing to you.

We also welcome you to attend one or more of our strategic seminars, workshops, camp meetings, and conferences.

We welcome initiatives from churches and event organizers to hold strategic events for the empowerment of God's people and the improvement of the general wellbeing of lives around the world. Feel free to let us know how we can work together for the advancement of God's Kingdom.

Visit our website or search online to learn more about additional materials from us to help you grow and prosper God's work beyond your time.

We pray that the Lord would continue to multiply His blessings on your life as you walk with Him for His glory, in Jesus' precious name!

ABOUT THE AUTHOR

Emmanuel Idu had a life-changing spiritual encounter in his teenage years and began public speaking at an early age. He has a strong apostolic voice and a respectable insight into the Bible, allowing him to communicate deep biblical principles in clear and simple language.

Apostle Idu speaks to a wide range of audiences at strategic events worldwide and serves as the Bishop and General Overseer of a growing number of churches.

Emmanuel is a gifted strategist, course developer, speaker, writer, and progress trainer. His unconventional mind has distinguished him as an advisor and a personal confidant to leaders around the world.

Mr. Idu is happily married to Irene, and they have two daughters, Caroline and Darielle.

www.ingramcontent.com/pod-product-compliance
Lightning Source LLC
LaVergne TN
LVHW011325080426
835513LV00006B/191